Assisted
Loving

# Assisted Loving

*True Tales of*
*Double Dating*
*with My Dad*

## BOB MORRIS

*An Imprint of* HarperCollins*Publishers*
www.harpercollins.com

Several names and identifying features have been changed to preserve anonymity. Also, for narrative flow and impact, some scenes have been compressed, with incidents and dialogue slightly heightened.

FIRST EDITION

Library of Congress Cataloging-in-Publication Data is available upon request.

ISBN: 978-0-06-137412-8

08  09  10  11  12  ID/RRD  10  9  8  7  6  5  4  3  2  1

*In memory of my parents*

# Acknowledgments

Thanks to Jonathan Burnham, Ellie Covan, Jane Friedman, Trip Gabriel, Rachelle Garniez, Gordon Greenberg, Kate Hamill, Josh Hecht, David Hirshey, Sylvia Kesman, Gillian Laub, Leila Hadley Luce, Bob Lupone, Jay Mandel, Marisa Acocella Marchetto, Jeff, Janet, Ian, and Maddy Morris, Amy Nederlander, Daryl Roth, Bonnie Siegler, Margaret Low Smith, Bernie Telsey, and Charlotte Wasserstein. And for being the Irving to my Jackie, Ira Silverberg, love of my life.

# Contents

**PART ONE:** Sunny Mourning

1. Grave Situation     3
2. Song in His Heart     19
3. Fa La La, etc.     32
4. Flori-Dada     37
5. Geriatrix     47
6. Cake, Rain     49
7. Hello, Eighty     55
8. Only the Lonely     68
9. Outdated     83
10. Bird in a Guilty Cage     86

**PART TWO:** The Comedy of Eros

1. Geriatrix (cont.)     95
2. Date Date Goose     99
3. Dog Date Afternoon     110
4. Gracie Gravlax     117
5. Dating Games     125

6. Regular Joe and Fifth Avenue Florence     133
7. Love's Loser's Lost     145
8. Road Trip     158

**PART THREE:** Reconstructive Purgery
1. New Year, New Hip     171
2. Rehab Horribilis     183
3. Back in His Saddle     195
4. Demolition Dating     199
5. Tawdry Palms     211
6. And Bobby Makes Three     225
7. Auld Lang Resigned     233
8. Auld Lang Realigned     240

**PART FOUR:** Love's Labors Won
1. Inspecting Doreen     255
2. Nice to Meet You     262
3. Florida with Feeling     269
4. End Where It Started     282

# PART I

# Sunny Mourning

## CHAPTER 1

# Grave Situation

t's a month after my mother has died, October 2002. My father and I have just pulled into the Mount Ararat Cemetery in Farmingdale, on the flat south shore of Long Island. We pass through iron gates under a Star of David and cruise past row after row of headstones that all look alike. We park and get out of his silver Toyota Avalon, slam the doors, and start walking. Dad is moving slowly. He needs another hip replacement. Not to mention a dry cleaner. His yellow cardigan is a fruit salad of stains. But I have to say, even if his walk is a little gimpy, he looks pretty good for someone close to eighty. Smooth tawny skin, silky silvery hair. Bodes well for me, I guess. Neither of us knows exactly where my mother's grave is. And men don't ask directions, even in cemeteries. So we wander, two lost boys, sneakers on grass, silently passing endless rows of the dead.

We finally find her between some Cohens and Blums. ETHEL MORRIS, the footstone reads, that's all. Well, she was a simple woman. A librarian with modest desires—a comfortable pair of shoes, the occasional bouquet of flowers on a holiday, a sing-along in the car, a half-price coupon for ice-cream cake from the supermarket. She wanted to see her husband and two sons happy even as she struggled in the last years of her life.

We stare at her name. It could be a moment to talk about her, to talk about any regret we might feel about not doing our best for her as she withered. Instead, Dad starts to hum, softly at first, then loud enough to drown out the roar of cars on the nearby parkways. "I miss singing with your mother," he says. "Even when we ran out of things to say to each other, we always had something to sing."

"I know," I say. "I know."

"This is one of her top ten favorites. Every time I come here I'm going to do another one just for her."

Then he clears his throat, and sings to her grave.

*I'll be loving you*
*Always,*
*With a love that's true*
*Always.*

He sings the whole song—slowly, wistfully—with white eyebrows arched upward, nostrils flaring, in a sweet crooner's tenor. I can feel my throat burning—the feeling you get when you're about to cry, and I swallow hard to stop it. I would never want to cry in front of my father. That would be so uncomfortable, I tell myself.

*Not for just a year,*
*But always.*

Now he's finished, and the sound of traffic and birds takes over while we stand, staring down at her, unsure what else to do. Some grass, palest green, is starting to sprout from the soil we shoveled in front of a small crowd last month on top of her coffin. It was a rainy funeral. The rabbi had put black ribbons on our lapels and we had to rip them—a gesture of traditional Jewish mourning. Was Dad looking more stricken or relieved as he stood there, the chief mourner? What about me? I admit to having felt, even three days after her death, a sense of exoneration. She had been sick for ten years with a rare, debilitating blood condition. Dad did what he could for her, driving her to doctors, helping her into the car, sticking around when his impulse was to flee the overwhelming sadness. But in the end, he was inadequate. And while I related to his need to keep enjoying life even as she suffered, I also resented him for it. My big brother, Jeff, resented him even more than I did. Dad wouldn't help her with her pills. He insisted on being out of the house for hours for bridge games, yet he wouldn't hire the help that would make our lives easier. He told me she was a lost cause. True as it was, it sounded so cruel. So there's an acrid, unspoken guilt we share now, here at the place where she rests. I stand over her, reading her name on the new bronze plaque in the ground.

### Ethel Morris

We shift on our feet, a father and son with everything to talk about and nothing to say to each other. Then Dad thinks of something.

"You know," he says, "I always liked this cemetery."

"Oh yeah?" I say.

Actually, I'm thinking as I look around that I don't care for this place at all. And I also don't like myself for thinking such a thing. But lately, this kind of snobbery has started taking up the parking space in my head where nicer thoughts should be. I can't stop myself from looking at this cemetery where my mother is finally resting in peace (from my father and me) and applying the same standards that I do to a hotel or restaurant. I think to myself that the location of this cemetery isn't genius. It's all wrong, in fact, sandwiched between two noisy roads. Who needs that? And the headstones of this cemetery are too much alike—new slabs of polished marble that aren't aged enough to have historical charm. They're all as evenly spaced apart and repetitive as the undistinguished homes in the nearby split-level development where I grew up, homes I was accustomed to as a child but now find embarrassing in their modesty. Some cemeteries are poetic and overgrown, with pretty hills, water views, and famously depressed poets buried beneath towering pines and elms. What does this cemetery have? Easy access to the Southern State Parkway?

"I have to tell you something important," Dad says.

"What's that?"

"There's a plot for you here, Bobby. I bought it years ago on my way to my Tuesday tennis game. So now you know you can be buried here with your mother and me when your time comes."

I nod. I'm touched at the sweetness of his gesture. But then, I'm ashamed to find myself thinking, *The last thing I want is to be buried on the south shore of Long Island for all eternity. Unless it's the Hamptons, of course.*

But what kind of son would say that?

"Um, that's so nice of you, Dad," I tell him. "But what about Jeff? He'll want to be buried here with you and Mom, too, won't he? Will there be room for all of us?"

"Your brother has a family of his own, Bobby, and they love Westchester," he says, as a groundskeeper drives by in a truck. "But *you*, since you're alone, and probably won't have a family of your own, I thought you'd want to be buried here with us."

It's a nice offer. And I know I should probably just thank him for the hospitality, then let him give me one of his father-son bear hugs he hopes will bond us. I mean, he's talking about wanting me at his side forever, in the hereafter, and I'm thinking of telling him I have other plans? Sure, my life has always been a little too busy to include him comfortably. But my death? There's every reason why I should just agree to his loving and lovely proposal. But I can't do it. I can't just say thanks and hug him back.

I'm forty-four years old, and I still don't know when to give my old man a break.

I don't say anything for a long while, just keep nodding over my mother's grave, and listening to the traffic with my lips firmly pressed together.

I am feeling something between aggravation and remorse.

Well, what can I say? This little visit from Manhattan, where I live the high-key, low-paying life of a minor style columnist at a major newspaper, is turning out to be the usual decathlon of challenges. I mean, last night, I step off the train in Babylon for a visit because Dad called to say he was lonely and needed some moral support. He's not at the station, late as usual. So I sigh and wait, watching everyone else drive off. Then, finally, he arrives, and I clear the papers and debris off of his passenger seat, sit down in his junk-strewn sedan, and get my favorite new white jeans soaking wet. Something sticky and most likely dietetic is seeping into my boxer shorts as he drives.

"What's on this seat, Dad?"

"Oh, I'm so sorry, Bobby, I forgot to clean up my Snapple."

We head for a bargain restaurant of his choosing. It's essentially a pizza parlor with plastic tablecloths, lit with fluorescent lights. I know I'm being ridiculous for paying attention to anything other than him, the old man who did his best to raise me. But I'm sorry. As the visitor who's gone to some trouble to get out here from the city, don't I have a say about where we eat? He wants to dine. I want to whine.

"Isn't there anywhere else, Dad?" My voice sounds like a child's.

"Just give this place a try, I guarantee you'll like it."

I don't know why I'd attempt to persuade him when I know he's so controlling. Why not just say, *Yes, fine, perfect choice!* Is it because of my own raging insecurities and disappointment at how my life has turned out? With no children of my own in middle age, let alone a spouse, I suppose I have to try to assert myself over *someone*. Am I treating my father's choice of a restaurant with the same controlling intensity my friends use to choose preschools and bar mitzvah bands?

Once we're seated, and he's ripping into the Italian bread in the plastic basket before us, I urge him to put his napkin in his lap, and he takes several cell phone calls from friends and bridge buddies. His ring tone, "The Mexican Hat Dance," seems to me to be the only politically incorrect ring tone I have ever heard. I should be amused.

"Hello, there," he says, as he always does. "Great to hear from you!"

Why can't he just put the phone away, focus on dinner, and have a meaningful conversation with me about his new life as a widower?

"Dad, I'm missing good parties in the city tonight to be with you," I say. "And you'd rather talk on your cell phone to your friends? Should I be insulted?"

"Don't be so sensitive. I'm just taking care of business. No big deal."

Driving in the car to the house, he is too consumed with a Mets game on the radio to talk. Nothing new. I shrug and put down my window, even though he prefers it up.

"I like the fresh air," I mutter. "Hope you don't mind."

We pull up to the Cape Cod house in our neighborhood by the bay. I get out of the car and stand in the driveway while Dad listens to the fourth inning. The old 1950s house—white shingles in need of painting, black shutters, the fading 509 at the door—has not changed my whole life. A stunted dogwood tree shudders, half naked in autumn. A harvest moon is rising over the water beyond the canal. The night is cool, quiet as it always is out here, except for some crickets. For a moment, everything slows—life expectations, all the opinions, my need to get this visit over with—and it all feels lovely.

But then I step inside and find that the house, spare in the modest decor my mother barely changed her whole life, has become his domestic Dumpster. On the Formica counters in the kitchen—half-eaten desserts, and his margarine tubs with bits of dried fruit soaking like science projects. Over the Jetsons swivel chairs, towels drying. Mail, brochures, and pages of coupons from local newspapers cover the white table like leaves on a lawn. The master bedroom is a weed-infested lot of dirty socks and underwear. Dad can't be bothered to pick up his clothes or throw away his junk mail. Or maybe he doesn't know how. Is he unmoored without a woman to cook, clean, and keep after him? Or is he suddenly having the time of his life, an old bachelor allowed to go hog wild in his own little Animal House, finally free to answer to no one but himself?

I don't know whether to laugh or worry. As a man living alone in my own apartment, I'm capable of an extreme mess myself. But never unhygienic like this.

I should not look in his study. But I do. There are mountains of papers—files, envelopes, bills—spilling out of his olive green filing cabinet, crowding the avocado green convertible couch, and colonizing the pea green vinyl recliner where my mother kept her legs up in her later years because it was too far for her to get to the den. Her whole life she lived in mortal fear of having to deal with his landfill of files—a paper trail to whatever assets they had, but also a toxic waste dump of endless entangling red tape.

"Honey," I remember her saying a little too assertively when he was watching a game on TV, "you promised to clean out your study today."

"Ethel, stop nagging me," he'd reply. "I'll do it when I'm good and ready."

Company would be coming, and she was mortified at the thought of someone opening that study door. "It looks like a hurricane hit that room," she'd say.

"It's my room, and I'll do whatever I want with it," he'd snap.

Sometimes, when he was feeling magnanimous, he'd agree to let her go in, and while he was at tennis, she'd try to clean up. She moved so cautiously she might have been wearing a Hazmat suit. Taking great care not to disturb his piling (rather than filing) system, she'd pick up the obvious useless detritus he'd amassed—and leave it in boxes on the curb. Later, when he was home, she'd be looking out their bedroom window and see him hunched over and collecting his things from her boxes to bring back inside, looking like something between a raccoon and a lunatic going through the trash.

It broke her spirit. But not her heart. She loved him, stubborn as he was.

"You couldn't clean up a little for me, Dad?" I'm saying now.

He shrugs. "I guess I could, but what's the point? You're family."

I'm not sure what to say to that. But I still want to have a moderately meaningful father-son conversation. I think we should check in with each other about what

it's like after a woman who loved us both so much has
left us. Does he have the same regrets I do? Does he
want to talk about how it feels in this big house alone
without her? I guess not, because he hobbles straight
back to his black recliner in the den, hits the remote
control, and turns to his Mets game on TV. I collapse
beside him on the off-white couch where my brother
and I sat on our mother's lap as little boys, waiting for
him to come home for dinner, always late from tennis.
We used to play a game from the window, guessing how
many cars it would be before his would appear. Dinner
was ready in the kitchen. There was nothing left to do
but wait. Mom held us close. The lights of cars would
come around the neighbors' pine trees. One, two, three,
four, five. No Daddy. Where was he? We worried. And
the numbers we guessed got longer as we got wiser to
his ways. But finally he'd arrive, so happy, so delighted
to be with all of us, not distracted or anxious the way
some fathers might have been. He never needed a drink.
Never needed a moment to himself. When he came in
that door, he kissed Mom with such vigor it made us
blush and then he was all ours, open-armed and smiling, a father who knew how to love his wife and family
without holding anything back.

I try to follow his baseball game, as I always have,
but I get bored. During commercials, Dad turns to me
to try to have a conversation. He wants to tell me about
his plans to sell the house. He wants to tell me about
his frequent-flyer miles and getting down to Florida for
free this winter. He wants to know if I've been in touch
with Mom's life insurance broker to collect on a sum that
isn't enough to bump me up to the next socioeconomic

bracket. Then the game comes back on, and he drops me like a bad date. This would be such a good time to turn over a new leaf with him, stop resenting and start accepting. What's the harm? I should watch the game. But I can't sit here any longer.

"Where are you going?" Dad asks.

"To bed, I'm tired," I mutter without turning around. "Good night."

Even with my mother finally gone from the house, my old upstairs bedroom feels the same. This is the quiet attic room I keep coming home to my whole adult life, from college on—always single or miserable in a relationship falling apart, often at odds with my career as well. Through the open window I hear a dog barking and the distant whistle of the train. It's Columbus Day weekend, and I imagine city people whizzing past our faceless suburb, dismissing it as they head for the glamorous resort communities farther east. Call me shallow, but I have always liked the Hamptons, with all the physical beauty and ugly behavior. My column in the paper often lampoons the pretty and privileged there, the ones at parties who look right through me and my oh-so-lackluster pedigree. They aren't nice people, they shouldn't be important to me, and yet I gravitate toward these types, seeking their compliments for my work and acceptance into their milieu. I wasn't cool in high school. It's alarming to think I'm still trying to make up for it now.

I brush my teeth in the dusty rose-tiled bathroom. The sink sits on crooked chrome legs. The lamps flanking the medicine chest are hopelessly kitsch. I put on my old pajamas from the top drawer of a dresser that's been there forever. I peel down a worn red bedspread to reveal the twin bed that has creaked ever since I jumped on it as a boy. The other bed, where my brother used to sleep, is empty. He has not slept in this room with me since he got married fifteen years ago. I've missed him ever since. How did he, a socially awkward young man, end up growing into himself, finding such an attractive wife, raising such lovely kids, and making such a rich and complete life for them all? Is it a failing of imagination to fall into lockstep with society as he did to create a family? Or is it an invigorating leap of faith? At least he's gone somewhere since adolescence. Where am I? Back alone in this bedroom, still waiting for life to begin. I turn out the lamp on the end table where I still have record albums from high school.

And soon I'm sleeping better than I do anywhere else in the world.

In the morning—*quel horreur*—there's only hazelnut nondairy creamer for the coffee, even though Dad knows I prefer real milk. The mug I pull off the shelf is so dirty I have to rewash it. Dad is spending far too long in the bathroom with a copy of *Tennis Week*, leaving me to wonder if we're ever going to get to the cemetery. Nothing quite stills him like a magazine on a toilet.

"Dad," I say outside his bathroom door. "What are you doing in there?"

"All right already," he says. "I'll be right out."

It's strange to be in this same spot in the front hall, where my mother used to stand her whole life, begging him to get out of that bathroom for fear of being late.

"I don't have all morning, Dad!"

"I said I heard you!"

As he puts on his cardigan, I wonder why have things gotten so peckish so fast? Death is supposed to have transformed us. They say that when it happens in your family, it's like something has changed in your life that's as monumental as the geography or climate. I think I want to feel that more potently. The loss of his wife of fifty years, my mother for almost as many, should be helping me put all my petty issues aside so we can finally be the easygoing father-and-son team we're meant to be. We have that potential to enjoy each other, I think. He doesn't just tolerate me. He respects me. And even if I can't quite respect him back, I'd like to be able to accept him more graciously. There are times I can almost feel it's about to happen. So what if he chose the Mets over me last night? So what if he scheduled a bridge game at the last minute so that we now have to rush the time we planned for the cemetery? And what's the big deal that he can't be bothered to clean out his car or kitchen for my oh-so-charitable visit? This is all so meaningless, so superficial, nothing that should get in the way of the all-encompassing affection a son should feel for his hapless, well-meaning father in his last years on earth.

Yet I keep feeling myself pulled back to the cynicism of adolescence.

Finally out of the house, we drive through the old hometown. Same old sprawl. Same old Catholic churches on every other block and looming sports fields—two worlds that excluded me and contributed to memories of high school alienation. By the time we pull up to Dad's bank at the shopping center I'm deflated. We are here to close one of Mom's savings accounts. My father wants to sign it over to me. It's a small amount of money I can use in my freelance life. He walks in, and the whole place is greeting him like a conquering hero. "Hello, Mr. Morris, how are you?"

"Hello, Linda," he calls out. "Hello, Debbie!"

"How you doing?"

"Great, I'm doing great," he says. "This is my son, Bob, the writer."

He introduces me to every employee in the bank as if he were something between a campaign manager and a publicist. He turned me into a quasi-celebrity here years ago by handing out clippings of all my columns and travel articles. It's very sweet, I have to say. But also embarrassing, especially because I'm not nearly as accomplished as I'd like to be. If I'd gotten as far in life as I'd imagined when I lived in this town, these people would know who I am without my father telling them. I force a smile. But no thanks, I don't want to chat with Annette, the assistant manager with the Dolly Parton cleavage. I just want to close a bank account, get out of here, and get to my mother's grave.

"Bobby," says Dad, with the stagy cordiality of a talk-show host, "why don't you tell Annette here what articles you're working on this week?"

"Nothing of interest right now," I say, as my foot taps the floor.

"Any celebrity interviews scheduled? Any travel stories?"

"No, Dad, nothing." My cheeks are starting to burn. I take a step away.

"Well, have you heard anything from Sarah Jessica Parker or Jennifer Lopez?"

"What? No! I'll see you in the car. Nice to meet you, Annette."

Outside, in the parking lot, he looks defeated. I feel prickly.

"Annette is a big fan of your column," he says, as he gets out his car keys and some old tissues from his pocket. "She was excited to meet you."

"Yes, because you bring her my clippings, right? You just like showing me off."

"What's wrong with that? I'm proud of you."

He blows his nose with a honk loud enough to stop traffic on Union Boulevard.

"Look, Dad, I don't feel like talking to strangers today, okay?"

"Just trying to pass the time," he says. "Nothing to get upset about."

"I know," I say as I pat his shoulder. "I know that."

In his car, while he listens to the news, my head starts throbbing—thud, thud, thud—as if it were a wall of one of the dilapidated handball courts where my brother and I practiced tennis as kids while he played all day on a public court. I smolder as he drives too slowly to make it through one traffic light, then another. Always the same story. Does every father have the ability to annoy a son so easily with his harmless habits? "Come on, Dad, focus," I sigh. "You can go faster."

"Please! Don't rush me, just let me drive."

I hate that it always comes to this. I wish I weren't so critical of his every foible, so anxious to bust him for every tiny thing he does wrong. And I'm ashamed of how often I think my life would be so much simpler without all the long-winded phone calls, tedious meals, and

inopportune trips he expects me to take to see him in
Florida each winter. I'm angry with the last person in the
world who deserves my wrath, and I know it.

So now here we are, standing at my mother's new
grave, where he has just sung to her so sweetly, and he
has just as sweetly offered me a chance to join both of
them here for eternity (his treat) because he doesn't want
me to be alone. And I know this is my chance to say yes
for once, to start over before we end, to hug my father, to
forgive my father for his imperfections, to forgive myself
for judging him so harshly, and to forgive the whole world
for everything I find so objectionable.

But that's not what comes out of my mouth.

"Listen, Dad," I say instead, "this cemetery is right
next to the parkway, and you know how I am about traffic
noise. I'm a very light sleeper. It's just not my scene."

"Suit yourself," he says, as he turns to head back to the
car. "Just thought I'd offer. You can always change your
mind."

## CHAPTER 2

# Song in His Heart

Who is Joe Morris? A seventy-nine-year-old man fully conversant with the idea of happiness, especially his own. A retired lawyer (and administrative law judge for the New York State Department of Motor Vehicles) of little ambition or taste who doesn't have an entitled bone in his body. His outfits—from the ski parka he used to wear around the house instead of a bathrobe to the gray vinyl loafers he used for tennis while he still played (and still wears today, even for dressy occasions)—are down-market at best. When you are as insecure as I am, you tend to believe that your father is a reflection of yourself. I want him looking sharp, and assess him with the eyes of a brutal teenager.

"Where did you get that?" and "Must we, Dad?" have been my laments for years.

Who is Joe Morris? He is the only real estate investor who ever *lost* money in the Hamptons. He is a man who would rather complicate than simplify. He has nineteen bank accounts and half a dozen partly organized bridge games that he has to monitor like an air traffic controller. He has discount cards from every oversize drugstore in America and frequent-flyer miles on a smorgasbord of airlines that don't add up to anything, but keep accumulating on beds, tables, counters, or anywhere but the wastepaper basket. He is a man who tapes tennis tournaments and basketball games while watching them on TV. He is a man who gleefully mixes his prescriptions as if they were sundae toppings, and pushes them on you every time you sneeze. That's because he likes to be useful and also have control of things. And when he sees someone like me, a little vulnerable and frustrated with life, it really revs his engine.

"Let me give you a bit of advice" is his clarion call.

Heaven help you if you're his partner at the bridge table. Early in my parents' marriage, when they still played together as partners, my father excoriated my mother so vociferously she turned bright red. She didn't answer back. But she vowed never to play on his side again. Instead, she'd have to serve as peacemaker between him and whoever was unlucky enough to be his partner.

Joe Morris is a man who became an orphan at ten years old. My aunt Sylvia, his impeccably dressed and stalwart older sister, tells me that living between the homes of grandparents upstate and cousins on Long Island made him feel lost growing up, confused about where he belonged. "He never quite knew where he should be," she says.

I wonder if losing both parents by the time he was ten makes him want to control as much of his life, including the people in it, as he possibly can. Maybe having no parents has also increased his need to be loved by as many strangers as possible. Is that why he talks to everyone and anyone he meets, even when they're clearly not in the mood? He thinks it will make you happy every time he offers you something to drink or eat—the half a Little Debbie crumb cake from his overstuffed glove compartment, for instance, or the cocktail he's invented of Amaretto and pineapple juice.

Years ago, when I was well into my thirties, unemployed, uncoupled, and living with my parents for a summer that lasted way too long, I was so bored that I went out to the driveway one day and inventoried his accumulation in the Chrysler Valiant he was driving at the time. In the front seat, I found a typed deposition from his law office, brochures from his tennis club, a schedule for a Chilean airline—although as far as I knew he wasn't planning to go to South America. Also: a scrap of paper from a Marriott (his favorite hotel chain) with some of his scrawl on it, an old wooden Wilson racket, and a visor from the tennis club at Century Village, the retirement community in Florida. There were tissues in a box marked up with more of his barely legible scrawl—notes for a legal case on one side and an idea for a song parody on the other. I found a worn paperback novel, *The Rabbi*, with a Nedick's coupon inside, and a wall calendar from the dry cleaner. Instead of cigarette butts in the ashtray, there were bank deposit envelopes. And wedged in by the emergency brake handle—a plastic cup with pencils, asthma inhaler, reading glasses, and a potpourri of pills, coins, and postage stamps.

I don't know why I did this inventory. Maybe I thought that the best way to face what was disturbing me was to look straight at it. That summer I had been reading some short stories by Tennessee Williams, whose relationship with his father was also strained. "You will begin to forgive the world," Williams wrote, "when you have forgiven your father." It made sense but seemed an unattainable goal. But I kept trying. Anyway, it had been a clean moment for his car, I realize now. The worst may have been in the 1970s, when it smelled like decaying flesh. A veal chop had been rotting in his tennis bag.

"Life with Joe is irritating, but never dull" is all my mother ever said.

She would know. She was the one who had to put up with the dinner guests he brought home from the tennis court without giving her warning. She was the one who had to be delighted when, without so much as an advance conversation, he brought home a German shepherd puppy one year and a calico cat the next. And when there was a sale at the local dollar store, suddenly all kinds of things would be crowding her front porch. To this day he marks them with return-address labels, just in case someone feels inclined to steal his white plastic chair or cheap folding umbrella.

My mother's sisters, Phyllis and Bev, still remember witnessing the aftermath of an incident twenty years ago, when he pocketed a bar of soap from Aunt Bev's condo in North Carolina. My mother chastised him gently for taking something that wasn't his.

"I'm warning you right now to leave me alone," he told her.

"I'll buy you your own bar of soap, honey," she said. "Just put it back."

"I'm going to divorce you, Ethel!" he roared as he stomped off to their car. Her two sisters watched with dropped jaws as she got in beside him. She was flushed with shame but stone-faced. He floored it in reverse and spun out of the parking lot, with my mother as his frightened hostage.

"All for nothing but a lousy bar of soap," my aunt Phyllis told me.

Maybe his hoarding of things, like his extreme friendliness, is also a result of the childhood. Finally, as an adult, he had a home and a car to call his own and colonize in his own way. I don't know why he's such a sloppy dresser, when Aunt Sylvia always shopped for him at the best stores when he was growing up. And I don't know why he's such a happy boor at dinner. His table manners are as questionable as his jokes. For instance:

*So the Pope and Bill Clinton both die at the same time and by some terrible mistake, the Pope ends up in hell and Clinton in heaven. When the mistake is found out, they run into each other while changing places. "How was hell?" Clinton asks the Pope. The Pope shrugs, winces, says, "Kind of hot, not so good. But how was heaven? I am so looking forward to being there. I have always wanted to meet the Virgin Mary." And Clinton looks at him, shakes his head, and says, "You're ten minutes too late."*

Joe Morris is a man who wanted to be a crooner his whole life. To this day he always has a song cued up in his heart, and like it or not, you're going to hear it, and like it or not, he's going to try to get you to sing along. For him there's no occasion that can't be sweetened by a song, just as there is no dessert that can't be improved with one of the packets of Sweet'n Low he keeps in his wallet. When my mother, who was pretty and curvaceous enough to be nicknamed "Yum Yum" in her twenties, told him she was pregnant with my brother in 1955, they were in a restaurant on Long Island. He walked up to the pianist, asked for the microphone, and started crooning. She was both mortified and delighted.

*Just Ethel and me*
*And baby makes three*
*That's living,*
*Long Island Heaven!*

Who is Joe Morris? A man who spent most of World War II performing little parodies of pop songs he wrote at his training camp in Amarillo, Texas. Then, the night before getting shipped off to Europe on a fighter plane, he ate six doughnuts and woke up with a stomachache that kept him from leaving the country.

"Wow, Dad, wasn't that kind of disappointing?"

"That assignment could have gotten me killed, so I was actually very lucky."

We are eating breakfast at his favorite diner on the highway around the corner from the old homestead. It's a month after our visit to the cemetery, Veterans Day, the day he got married in a modest family ceremony to my mother in 1951.

"So you never left the country during the war, Dad?"

"I finally got sent to Iceland as it was ending."

"Iceland? All your friends were in Normandy, right? Didn't that bother you?"

"Why should that bother me?"

"Didn't you want to be a hero, Dad?"

"Who doesn't? But if I had been, then maybe there wouldn't be any me, and then there wouldn't have been any you, so things kind of worked out for the best, right?"

He slurps his tea with orange juice, chews his pancakes with his mouth open. This is no power breakfast. The coffee in this Greek diner is anemic, the French toast soggy, and the view of the parkway entrance across the highway dreary. But to him, this is all perfect. It could be breakfast at the Regency or the Ritz.

"I can't tell you how much I love this diner," he says. "Try the blueberry syrup. If you add just a teaspoon of orange juice, it cuts the sweetness."

Is there something to be said for being so content? He is essentially a happy man. Or is it just that he can't be bothered to aspire to anything more than this? My whole life is about trying to leave a mark on the world in ways he never could. And my past few years have been consumed with failed pitches and proposals. I want things that are so far out of reach and beyond his imagination that I live in a perpetual state of aspiration. And what does Dad want? A toasted bagel, a good duplicate bridge game, and for me to enjoy his latest concoction.

"Um, no, thanks, Dad," I say. "I'll pass on the syrup."

He shrugs it off—he's used to my dismissals—but I can see he's disappointed.

We leave the diner, after his long conversation with a waitress. There is no man on earth who loves talking to strangers as much as him. He has what used to be called a hotel face—that's the guy who either knows or wants to know everyone in the lobby.

It's nippy outside today, early winter, when the wind off

the bay makes the south shore of Long Island damp and unwelcoming. Dad hates this cold, and his migratory hormones are rising. He's counting the days until his return to Florida. In the parking lot, he fishes car keys out of his pocket, bringing up a half-sucked throat lozenge.

"Do me a favor, Bobby," he says, as he hands me the keys. "Get the car for me."

"Why, Dad?"

"I'd rather not walk in the cold. My hip is bothering me."

"Oh, come on," I say. "The car's right there, just a minute's walk. You have to walk a little. You can use the exercise. It's good for your circulation."

"Please, Bobby. Just get the car for me. Why do you have to argue?"

Why do I have to argue? It's just that he can be so lazy. Joe Morris is a man who refuses to *walk* anywhere. He once refused to get out of the car in California to take in a redwood forest I desperately wanted him and my mother to see.

"I can see from here," he said.

"Dad, please get out. I promise it'll be worth it."

"You go ahead. I don't feel well."

"Really? What's the matter, honey," my mother asked.

"I'm nauseous. I think it was the drive up here," he moaned.

"Bullshit," I said. "You just don't want to walk. Come on, Mom, come with me."

"I think I'll stay here with Dad," she said.

"No, you won't. Come with me."

I'd been living in mellow central California for a year, meditating, taking the kind of drugs that were supposed to give you some detachment and perspective in the late

1970s, before Prozac totally removed bad moods from the culture. But I was too angry to accept no for an answer. I walked her to the beginning of a path into the forest, well marked and unthreatening in the filtered light of a California afternoon. She hesitated.

"Come on, Mom," I said.

"I don't want to, honey. I'm worried about Dad."

"He's fine."

"It's not nice to leave him behind in the car."

This was nothing new in our little Oedipal triangle. By early adolescence, I wanted her love as much as he did, and as the soulful son with artistic aspirations, I wanted to lead her to the enriching experiences he couldn't provide.

"Let's go back, honey," she said.

"Okay, but first I want you to look up," I said.

"Why?"

"Just look up."

She did. Up above, the branches of redwoods rose into infinity, catching the sunlight like windows in a cathedral.

"See that, Mom? See how the branches are moving?"

"Oh, look," she whispered. "It's like they're praying."

It was a delicious moment. I had rescued her from him and his limiting ways. Not that she was so expansive. She was limited, too, the one who worried in contrast to his freewheeling spontaneity. She fretted each time I wanted to change jobs. She canceled plans because of snow flurries. She worried too much about the future. The wind increased, the trees swayed. Suddenly, Mom turned to go, breaking the spell. I stood, stock-still.

"You're going back to the car?" I called out.

She turned. "I have to. You stay as long as you like. We'll be waiting."

I let out a sigh. My father had won. She was his captive. I still don't know why I dragged him to that redwood forest. What was I thinking? The only thing nature does for him is make him sneeze. Mountains? A little too high. Beach? Too much sand for his taste. He has no idea what is good for him. And even though he's old now, that doesn't mean he's wise. His Pavlovian response to my message machine beep is a captain's log of superficialities—what he ate for dinner, where he played bridge, the plot of the movie he just saw, that goes on and on from here to eternity, or at least until his voice is finally unceremoniously cut off by the beep. My mother tried to tell him not to leave long, rambling messages. He told her to stop nagging him. He's telling the same thing to me now, in the parking lot of this diner, where he is refusing to walk to his car. I stomp off to get it with the angry little steps of a five-year-old who can't have his way.

Are we going to be working this same material until he dies? If he goes from loving to furious around me from time to time, it's only because he doesn't know how else to respond to my nagging and cynicism.

We drive to the train station, passing the endless athletic fields of my youth. By the age of ten, I wanted my father to be like the other jock fathers in our community. He was great at singing in the car, teaching me jokes, and helping me make funny home movies. But I could see he was as uncomfortable as I was with a football or basketball. It took some effort to keep from being bullied in gym class. Well, like father, like son. He liked Ping-Pong. He liked tennis. Wimp sports.

When I was twelve, I was on the court with him at our beach club for a father-and-son end-of-summer tourna-

ment. It was a sticky night, and the bay smelled of sea-
weed. The lights were on, glaring white mercury beams
overhead that might have been towering over a prison.
My tennis whites were my uniform. I felt totally trapped.
I wanted to be home watching the new fall sitcoms. It
was, after all, the debut season of *The Partridge Family*. We
weren't going to win this match. Why did I have to bother
going through such motions? I moped around the court,
rolling my eyes. My father had an oddly good game based
on annoyingly high lobs, drop shots, and dinks. Sometimes he'd even switch hands when he played, totally
confounding opponents as he sent balls sailing slowly
past them. He was always an encouraging and gentle
partner. "Move up! Bend your knees! Watch your alley!
That a boy!" He meant well. But his unsolicited coaching
drove me crazy. I kept double-faulting.

"Throw the ball higher," he said, with increasing intensity.

"Get back up to the net, Dad," I snapped.

He would not. He needed to stand on the baseline and
give me pointers. Our opponents were waiting, and so
was the crowd of people watching us from lawn chairs.

"Leave me alone, and just play," I said in a voice waver-
ing between boy and man.

"I will when you stop double-faulting. Give me a nice
high toss on your serve."

I did and served better. We won a point. At the next,
we found ourselves together at the back of the court, an
awkward place. A ball came right to my backhand.

"Got it!" I called.

He poached it right out from under me and lobbed it
too shallow. Faster than you could say "bonk," an over-

head smash humiliated both of us. Why didn't he let me take that shot? The next thing I did—and I still see this in slow motion—was rear back and, with my well-honed backhand after years of lessons, nail him hard with my racket right in the center of his right arm.

"Oh!" the crowd gasped.

"Ow!" Dad cried. He dropped his racket and went hopping around the court like a turkey full of buckshot. More gasps from the onlookers. "Oh my goodness," said Selma Weinstein as she stood up from her beach chair in shock. Mary De Luca put out her Kent in her ashtray and called out, "Joe, are you all right?"

He gestured at her with his hand, as if to say, Get away! I'm fine.

Sadly, I can't even remember feeling concern for him. Just embarrassment at his reaction, not my behavior. I had not hit him that hard. And it was with a wooden racket, after all, not one of the new metal ones coming into vogue at the time. Why couldn't he just smack me back in retaliation and tell me we were going home? Maybe if he'd been a tougher guy, I wouldn't have taken such advantage of his gentleness.

"So then, nothing else to report?" Dad is asking at the traffic light near the station. Breakfast is already repeating on me with the unpleasantness of childhood memories.

"No interesting trips planned? Anything new with your social life?"

"Social life, Dad? What does that mean?"

"I don't know. Romance, the usual."

"Um, no, but thank you for asking"

"Okay, fair enough," he says as we roll into the station. My train is already on the track. How many times have we barely made it to a train because he is so habitually late? How many times has he kept me waiting here when I'd arrive from the city? Is this why I'm always so late myself? I see him and am terrified he's the man I will become. And because I'm good at blaming, I resent him for the bad habits he's passed on to me.

"My train's already up on the track," I say, interrupting the plans he's trying to make for next weekend. "I've got to go, Dad. Talk to you later." I grab my bag and jump out of his car, slam the door, and run for the train, suddenly feeling alive again to the possibilities of my city life far from this stifling suburbia.

"See you, Dad!" I run and make the train as the warning bell rings and the doors close. From my window I watch his car leaving the parking lot and making a left turn toward the home where he now suddenly lives alone.

It is only as the train picks up speed that I realize I didn't thank him for breakfast or extend a hand to him to say good-bye.

## CHAPTER 3

# Fa La La, etc.

Holiday time is always a good run for me, party-wise. Without the pressing concerns of getting home for Christmas stocked with presents, I'm free to flit from one overreaching event to the next. And when you traffic in my socially superficial style world, the invitations keep coming. Staff party for the posh travel magazine where I'm a contributing editor. Annual blowout in Soho given by the hipster president of a big publicity agency. I am booked every night in the middle of December, showing up in the red plaid Christmas pants that I hope people know I'm wearing with irony. Other nights it's all about the black velvet jacket that reeks of all the sophistication my upbringing lacked. Usually, I arrive alone at parties, with nobody on my arm. And that's okay because I'll know all kinds of people once inside. These are my party friends—journalists, stylists, publicists (but no socialists) with whom I'm intimate at the least-intimate occasions—the hot dressers and hot nobodies, like me, who are best friends for a few hours once a year.

"Bob, that last column was a riot!"

"Bob, you're so fabulous, why don't you have someone?"

I rarely answer. It's Christmas Eve now, and I'm with my pal Marisa's family in New Jersey. Marisa is a bling-dressing, high-stepping cartoonist whose vixens have blown-out hair and blown-up breasts. We're taking a cigarette break outside in the misty December air. My problem with Marisa these days is how preoccupied she is with her new love, Silvano, the owner of an important Italian restaurant. It's been hard adjusting to her recent infatuation. Just last fall, when she was complaining about how he flirts too much with the beautiful women who accost him in his restaurant, I told her to let him go.

"Love is as overrated as Tuscany," I said. "And so is marriage."

"You're just jealous I have a boyfriend, Bob," she snapped.

"Well, don't be looking for an engagement ring is all I'm saying. And for God's sake, don't be giving up your apartment just because you're shacking up with him."

"I can't believe you're so cynical about love," she said.

I can't either. But since then, her relationship has solidified, and I have learned to curb my cynicism, even though I still mock her for being at his beck and call. She's happy—she's found someone who makes her laugh all the time. And deep down I know she's right—I am jealous.

Marisa's parents are pleasant people with a modern 1970s ranch. They are as proud of her as my father is of me. Her art is all over their walls. But she doesn't seem embarrassed by that. In fact, she seems completely at ease in her childhood home. Her sister is here with her husband and child. It doesn't bother me to be the lone single person at the table. And I'm not at all surprised when, after dinner, Marisa announces that she and Silvano are getting engaged. Like everyone else at the table, I make a big noise of congratulations. Raising a glass, I say, "I couldn't be happier for you, babe." But driving home alone past the competitive Christmas lights of the deep Jersey suburbs, I let out a sigh. "Well, so much for her," I mutter. One more friend lost to love and marriage. I've been watching my friends march off into the battlefields of love for years now, and I'm always on the sidelines, waving good-bye.

When I get back to the penthouse of my brother and family, where I usually stay alone for the holidays so I can pretend to be wealthy, the phone rings. My brother is calling from Palm Beach. Every year, he makes it a point to drop in with his family and play the good son, before heading farther south to the Caribbean, where the weather is much better. He's staying at The Breakers this year. Florida has been cold and rainy. But he is enduring it so Grandpa Joe can see his grandchildren. I know my father appreciates their visit. But this year he hasn't been around to dote much.

"He blew us off for brunch today," my brother's telling me. "Can you believe that?"

"What was his excuse?"

"Who knows? I bet it was a bridge game."

I laugh. "He ditched you for bridge?"

"Yup. We use up half our Christmas vacation to be with him in fucking Florida, where it's cold and rainy, and he'd rather play bridge than see us. He's too busy running around to spend time with his own grandchildren."

I'm thinking that would be fine with me. How much of the old man does he want to see anyway? How much driving around in his car seeing the nonsights? But my brother doesn't think that way. To him, it isn't about what fun he can have with my father. It's about the appropriate face time a family should have together—obligation and respect. He's in Florida, thinking that this would be the year to huddle together, think about Mom, mourn, and heal. But Dad plays ditchy-do.

"Are you going to tell him you're disappointed?" I ask.

"What good would that do," he says. "If he doesn't want to talk about Mom, it's his problem."

"Well, it's nice you're down there," I say. "You're doing the right thing."

"Yeah," he says, "but I can't wait to get out of here to-morrow."

Frustrating as he can be at times, with the expectations he has for impeccable behavior from all of our family, Jeff is a good man. And I miss him now. I miss his good-natured wife, Janet, and the children, too. It's so quiet in this apartment without all of them. I'm used to being here when my cerebral niece and rollicking nephew are all over me. I'm used to being the crazy bachelor uncle who blows in to entertain the family with irreverent commentary, and makes every birthday party into a Vegas floor show. Just as my brother and his wife depend on me to spice up the conversation and get them reservations at tricky restaurants, their children depend on me to be the naughty entertaining uncle. And I depend on them for the intimacy that comes when you read children stories at night, hold their hands while crossing the street, sit them on your lap and make funny noises into their ears. They are as much my children as I'm ever likely to have in life. I live for their giggles. But right now I have this elegant penthouse that's usually so full of their laughter all to myself. All my friends are out of town somewhere fabulous. My father is having fun in Florida. Me? I'm here feeling like the tired and lonely old man he's supposed to be. The Empire State Building is lit up red and green. The stars are out over the city. Silent night. Silent week. And that's okay. I'd rather be alone than tangled up with someone who isn't just right for me. New Year's Eve is coming. I don't have a date. Nothing new. It's fine. Alone is fine.

## CHAPTER 4

# Flori-Dada

P alm Beach International Airport is clean, manageable, and suburban, just the way my father likes his
life. It's January now, four months after my mother
has died, and with the lonely holidays behind me, I'm
making one of my winter visitations when airfare is
cheap. It's a strange feeling, knowing my mother won't
be at the airport to meet me. Sometimes I miss her. Most
of the time, now, I am relieved not to have to worry about
her failing health. It surprises me how often she is out of
my mind completely.

With carry-on bag on my shoulder, I emerge from the
jetway, passing the usual herd of white hairs. Ladies in
sequin sweatshirts. Men in windbreakers and baseball
caps. All in every shade of pastel imaginable. It's a flock
of snowbirds thick as pigeons. They are all waiting for

their children, grandchildren, anyone young to get off the plane from New York. These migratory retirees—white and middle class—number nearly a million in Florida. They are aggressive about their pursuit of the good life, and proud to show their kids the orange tree in the backyard, the alligator in the lake by the golf course, and to gift them with the warmth of the sun. As they greet their cherished visitors at the airport, they beam with pride. Yet there's desperation in their eyes, I think. Is it reasonable to expect so much pleasure from your children? Is it reasonable to expect anything but the same old patterns of behavior from parents?

I step out onto the sidewalk and here's something new: the front of Dad's car is falling off. Half of the fender is mashed in and hanging off like it's just had a stroke or been stricken with Bell's palsy. The left side is steaming and hissing in the airport parking lot like a collapsed soufflé. I was planning on saving money on a rental by using his car while down here. I always stay with him because hotels are very expensive. The whole point was to get in some face time with both him and the sun without paying for much except airfare. The freelancer son takes a holiday. Now I won't have any wheels to use to escape him. I tell myself to stay pleasant, avoid confrontation.

"What happened, Dad?"

"I hit the median."

"Why?"

"I wasn't paying attention, that's all."

"Don't tell me you were talking on your cell phone."

"I was calling to check your flight status."

"Or were you answering a call from any one of your

friends? I told you to stop answering that phone when you're driving. You're going to have your license revoked. Imagine not having a car around here! What would you do, Dad?"

"Please, Bobby, don't start nagging at me. You just got here."

This is not good, not the plan at all, to start off so poorly. We've had so many awful fights down here in the past. Always about control. We both have very firm ideas of how things should be done. Where to eat and what time, for instance. The volume of the TV in the living room. Sliding doors to the balcony opened or closed? How strong should the coffee be? Important things, the stuff of life. Once, when my mother was still alive, Dad and I fought so hard about something so minute it seems absurd to describe it (the proper exit from a mall, okay?), and I actually threw his backseat car door open on Federal Highway—this was around midnight—and told him to pull over so I could get out and walk to a hotel. He told me he was sorry I had come to visit. I told him to fuck himself, all this unfolding right in front of my mother, who never swore and hated seeing her "boys" fight. Big drama over nothing. But uncontrollable as the weather.

According to a therapist whom I was talking to at a bar down here, children do tend to get into conflicts while visiting their snowbird parents in Florida. It's a combination of factors. Personal space issues for one, agendas for another. The kids want to get to the beach. The parents, who never set foot on a beach, want them home early so they can take them to early-bird dinner specials. They want to advise their children on how to raise children.

Their children want them to butt out. They want to buy their grandchildren ice-cream cones, a deadly idea in an era of parents obsessed with childhood obesity. Control, control, control. Other than incest and alcohol, is there anything more disruptive to family dynamics? One friend of my parents, a perfectly nice, laid-back woman, had a daughter-in-law who didn't like to see her having a couple of cocktails before dinner. So the daughter-in-law stopped bringing the grandchildren to visit. It was devastating and punitive. "She was drinking," my mother explained at the time, "because her daughter-in-law was making her so anxious."

Florida, in other words, can be a multigenerational mosh pit.

So why would anything go according to my carefully laid plans on this trip?

"We can still drive this," Dad says as we pull out of the parking lot. "No problem."

We approach the airport spur, with the front of his car rattling and smoking. Soon a distinct odor of burning—Toyota Teriyaki—permeates the air. People are driving past, giving us looks. My mood has gone murderous. The car seems to be getting worse by the minute. The temperature gauge is rising to high. I can't take my eyes off it.

"Dad, we aren't going to make it to your apartment," I say. "It's ten miles away."

"Oh, yes, we are," he says. "I can call Triple A from there."

"The engine's overheating. It's about to catch fire. Pull over."

"Not necessary. This is my car. I know what I'm doing."

"Are you crazy? Pull over right now or you'll end up getting us killed."

We are in the middle of the little city of Palm Beach now, the billion-dollar sandbar I find so appealing. I love that he has made his winter habitat on the edge of such elegance. But I hate that his middle-brow silver sedan is now smoking and making a total spectacle of us at a red light on South County Road, within sight of two upscale restaurants and The Breakers hotel. A headband-wearing blonde in the palest blue cocktail dress crosses with her white poodle in front of us. She gives us a look that is both concerned and condescending.

"There's a service station right here, Dad. You have to pull in."

"I'll do what I want. Don't tell me what to do."

"I will tell you what to do since you have no idea what you're doing."

Mad as it is, I grab the wheel and steer it to the right. He's about to fight me when his cell phone starts ringing, or perhaps I should say singing. His natural tendency to answer a call in any situation takes over. He grabs his phone from his shirt pocket, letting me guide the car in as he applies the brakes and turns off the burning engine.

An attendant comes and looks at the broiling, hissing mess, shaking his head. "What happened?" he asks.

I just shrug and point to Dad, on the phone.

"Hello, Edie," he's cooing. "Marvelous to hear your voice! What a thrill!"

Edie?

Later, over dinner (next to the service station) at Chuck and Harold's, one of the more pleasant restaurants on our regular list, he explains: "Edie lives down the road. I met her at a bridge game last year, and we played well together. She's a terrific partner, and very pleasant to be with. A real friendship developed. Strictly platonic."

"I certainly hope so," I say evenly. "Mom was still alive last year."

"But she wasn't able to get out much," he says.

I order another martini. What is going on here exactly?

An hour later, Dad's car is declared out of commission. So a taxi takes us back to his apartment. It's on Ocean Boulevard in a white wedding cake of a building called The President, sitting between the intercoastal waterway and the ocean. The owner, Dad's landlord, has decorated it in a tasteful array of whites. The water view is very pleasant. Aunt Sylvia lives upstairs. She dresses like everyone else in this building, treating life as an occasion to look your best—women in pumps, men in sports jackets for brunch. Here life is not about sweatshirts and sneakers, and I like that. My mother never did. And my father's essentially oblivious. He dresses how he wants.

The last time I was here my mother was still hanging on after five years of struggle. I can still see her everywhere in this apartment. There are even some leftover cans of Ensure, her dietary supplement, in the cupboard. Here's the balcony where she used to hobble out in her housedress to watch me play tennis down below with Dad's friends. Here's the door that knocked her down in a fierce wind and ended up leaving her covered in bruises. She was so helpless. It was hard, watching her in her hopelessness. It was even harder seeing her thin, bruised arms and neck because she dressed in the most unflattering T-shirts. One day I convinced her to come downstairs to be with me on the dock. She sat in silence, her skeletal face sharp as a hatchet.

This was not the mother I knew, the one who was so easy to amuse.

"You know, Mom, we all feel bad that you're so unwell," I told her. "But it's a sin to despair. Did you know that? I looked that up and found it in the Bible."

"I look terrible," she said. "My spleen is so enlarged I look pregnant."

"But what is the point of being so down? You're not in pain, are you?"

It wasn't a fair question. Why should she cheer up at sixty-eight years old, with mortality hanging over her, years before it was due? She shook her head, thought for a moment. The wind whipped her thinning hair and slacks on the reeds that were her legs. Her neck was like a stalk sticking out of her T-shirt. Why couldn't she dress up a little?

"Well, how about this? I won't complain if you won't criticize," she said.

"Okay, but I just have to tell you one thing, Mom."

"What, dear?"

"You could use some new shirts."

"Oh no, honey. Please don't start nagging about my clothes. I know I'm not stylish enough for you. I never have been. Why can't you accept that?"

In a way she was right. A mother isn't someone you can decorate according to taste, like an apartment. On the other hand, she is with you for life, isn't she?

"It's not about fashion, Mom," I persisted. "When you get older, you can't wear T-shirts and sweatshirts like that. It isn't flattering, especially when your frame is so thin. You need shirts with collars, sleeves, and structure. It will make you feel better about yourself, I promise. And what's with the hairnets? Aren't those for bed?"

"My hair has gotten so thin," she said as she touched it, yellow and wispy as sea grass blowing in the warm, salty wind. "When I step outside, it always gets messed."

"So let's see if we can get you some hats, okay? Please?"

"Bobby, what's the point?"

"Why not? What else do we have to do? It'll be my treat."

"Oh, all right. If you insist," she said as she stood up. "Take me to Macy's!"

So I did. In slow motion, we traversed a busy mall in Boynton Beach. And in the women's department, with salesclerks looking at me suspiciously, as if I were a bossy stylist from hell, I found the half-sleeve blouses I imagined for her and bought them in several colors. Then she tried on hats that looked ridiculous. But she ended up laughing at her reflection in the mirror for the first time in years. And when we got back to the apartment, she tried everything on with the kind of energy I didn't know she had anymore. For a woman who always said that clothes didn't matter to her, those new blouses were making her feel better than all the pills in her medicine cabinet.

"Thank you, my little personal shopper," she said.

I can still feel the touch of her lips on my forehead.

It's morning in the apartment now, and I'm about to make Dad some French toast using Mom's old recipe.

"So, Dad, Edie, huh?" I'm asking as I break eggs.

"Yes, and she's great."

"I was just thinking, is it a little early to be running around with another woman? I mean, it's just a few months since Mom died."

"It's not that serious," Dad says. "Edie's not available all that often anyway. But when she is, we have fun. She's the nicest woman I've met down here. Just a gem."

As I shake my head in mild disdain (*Kids these days!*) his phone rings. It's Edie. Thirty years fall off his face. His eyes get big as Alka-Seltzer tablets.

"Edie! I thought you were busy! No, I have no plans. I'd love to!"

The next thing I know, the French toast is languishing upstairs and I'm standing in his parking lot watching him get into Edie's silver Lexus for a bridge game in Delray Beach, thirty miles away. She rolls down her window to look me over. She is silver-haired, carefully tanned, lipsticked, and wearing what looks like a Rolex on her wrist. Not pretty, but nicely put together. "You have such a handsome son," she purrs. "And Joey, he looks just like you!" Then she blows me a kiss, rolls up her window, and drives him away. I watch her make a fast hard right turn onto Ocean Boulevard. Then I stand immobilized, eating their dust, a little in shock. For a moment there's no traffic and I hear the ocean. I hear gulls calling out, too, in mocking tones. Are they laughing at me? I came all the way down here to visit my dad, and he just ditched me for an air-kissing seductress in a luxury sedan? Don't get me wrong. I'm happy to have the day to myself. But I also have—as I stand in the sun in front of his building—an entirely unexpected feeling of emptiness.

I call my brother in New York, with the news flash.

"There's a woman named Edie in the picture," I say.

"You're kidding."

"That explains why he didn't have time for you when you were down here."

"Who is she?"

"All I know is she drives a silver Lexus that matches her hair. Three and a half months after Mom died, and Dad appears to be dating. Is this appropriate?"

"I don't know," Jeff says. "But since when has Dad been appropriate?"

## CHAPTER 5

# Geriatrix

nformational interlude. Here's something I never knew before. Or let me put it another way. Here's something I never had to think about until now: the Census Bureau estimates that 80 percent of all healthy widowers remarry, and many more end up in live-in relationships soon after a wife dies. There are no figures for senior dating or, as my dad calls it, "keeping company," but ask boomers these days and they will tell you they have or know of an elderly parent who is reentering the dating game after being widowed. Men like my father have the demographics in their favor. There are three women available for every one of them, a virtual sample sale for those energetic enough to shop; and with longevity what it is today, not to mention pharmaceuticals, many are. To make it even easier for the men, they have no trouble dating younger women, while the overwhelming majority of widows tend to end up with men older than themselves due to the long-standing societal norms that even Demi Moore can't undo.

One reason for men turning to dating soon after losing their wives? They enjoyed marriage the first time around. Another? They're incompetent. "Babies," one woman called them in an article I clipped on widowers and dating. In addition to being incapable of going to dinner alone (not necessarily the case with their busy female counterparts), men don't like to come home to an empty house or do housework. They're not just looking for love, they're looking for lunch. Senior women, meanwhile, find it liberating to be free of the responsibilities of marriage and caregiving. They are more likely to be good at maintaining social networks that don't even include men. Men who have lost their wives, on the other hand, are less adept at creating new social lives for themselves after so many years as half of a couple. So rather than spend a lot of time mourning, the way widows do, they get busy. As an old saying suggests, when there's a death, women mourn and men replace. After a few weeks of not terribly expressive grieving, the men can be ready to move on. And that's great, but what are the kids supposed to think the first time they see a freshly widowed parent in a car driving off on what appears to be some kind of date? And, more urgently, what the hell are they supposed to do?

CHAPTER 6

# Cake, Rain

P.S. 27 is a public elementary school in Red Hook, a housing-project neighborhood in Brooklyn that is not near any subway stop. It's so inconveniently located that I get sent out there in a chauffeur-driven town car when I make my four volunteer visits each winter. The organization that sends me pays for the car, an amenity that may seem counterintuitive to altruism, but works fine for me. It also helps that it's a late-morning gig, so I don't have to get up too early to make my contribution to society. As the author of one out-of-print children's book—about a privileged little Fifth Avenue kitty with serious family issues—I am part of an "authors read aloud" program.

It's a rainy Wednesday in February, six weeks or so after last seeing my father, when I get out of the car. Inside the school I sign in for a security guard. The fluorescent lights cast a harsh glow. The halls of the school are an institutional mint green. In the stairwells, there's Cyclone fencing. Some children I pass in the corridors recognize me from previous visits and they yell and wave.

For someone so free of responsibility, volunteering in schools provides both real meaning for me and also, let's be honest, something to brag about at dinner parties. My mother was always proud of me for my volunteer work. Oh, she worried about my going into dangerous neighborhoods, but she couldn't help but be encouraging. She was a volunteer for years. She would read to people in a nursing home on Long Island and lead book discussions. I prefer to volunteer with children. I play ukulele, sing silly cat songs, read my book, and talk about writing.

I love an audience. Even second-graders will do.

Today, I'm not feeling so inspired. It's my birthday, forty-five years old, and it does occur to me that, despite my ambition, I may be a little old to get much further ahead in life. There has not been another children's book, let alone a series. My style column in the paper isn't turning into a springboard for world media domination either. The other problem with my birthday, and I try not to let this bother me all that much, is that it falls on the day before Valentine's Day. So it's a double-barreled occasion for self-reflection.

Mrs. Stark's classroom is on the third floor, across from the drinking fountain. It's my second visit this winter. A sign on her door says, WELCOME AUTHOR BOB MORRIS! I open it and see a classroom full of faces focused on writing in workbooks. There are art and science projects all over the room. Mrs. Stark is a tough-talking young woman with a chipped tooth and a Brooklyn accent. She has what it takes to keep an overcrowded classroom in control, which seems to be, above all else, laser-sharp purpose and a sense of humor. She makes what I do for a living look like recess.

"There's a chair for you there, Mr. Morris," Mrs. Stark says.

I sit in an old tattered reading chair by the window.

"Okay now, class, stop writing," Mrs. Stark says. "One, two, three!"

And just like that, they come to attention at their little desks.

"Look who's here," she says. "What do we say to our guest?"

"Good morning, Mr. Morris!" they call out in unison.

The enthusiasm is heartening. I must have done something right on my first visit.

"Now, class, I want you to take your things and find a seat—quietly—on the rug. No pushing. And leave Mr. Morris some room. Can you do that, please?"

With a minimal amount of fuss, they scramble to sit cross-legged all around me, vying for the spaces right under my feet. They stare at my ukulele. They work to sit up as straight as they can. They aren't rich, but they are richly accessorized, with light-up sneakers, vivid Sponge Bob and Simpsons sweatshirts, and all kinds of plastic jewelry and geegaws in their hair. The new maximalists. They settle on the floor into a squirming, expectant mass, and Mrs. Stark calls them to attention again from her desk.

"Mr. Morris, before you begin, we have something we'd like to say to you."

"What's that?" I ask.

"Class? What do we have to say? One, two, three!"

There is a beat, about the length of time between light-
ning and thunder. Then, in perfect unison, they scream:
"Happy birthday, Mr. Morris!"

Their delivery is kind of primal. And my response is,
too. Tears fill my eyes.

"Now, class, starting with Juan," Mrs. Stark says, "bring
your things up to Mr. Morris." One at a time, they shyly
step up to me with handmade birthday cards.

I shake each hand and make a fuss over each card.
When they are finished, Mrs. Stark leads them in the
birthday song. When it comes time for me to sing my
own songs back to them, they are watching me so atten-
tively, so happy to have me here, that I lose control of my
voice for a moment.

I leave the school glowing, thoroughly pleased with
myself. In the town car back to Manhattan, instead of checking my phone messages, I read each birthday card again,
feeling a little like my parents must have felt when I made
them cards for every birthday and anniversary. "You're
funny, Bob Morris," says one from a boy named Angel. "You
are my favorite author," says one from a girl named Janelle.
This is what I call a haul. A good birthday.

I haven't had many meaningful birthdays. My fortieth
was pretty good. But that's because I was in love. I flew
into L.A. to be with a new beau, named Jack. He picked
me up at the airport, ruddy and rugged in corduroy shorts
and rain boots. We drove to the organic market, then to
his apartment, where he made an organic dinner. We had
not been dating long. It was my first time in his dark and
cramped home. I wish I hadn't studied his bookshelves

so carefully. They were full of self-help authors and New Age tomes.

At midnight, he presented me with a small box. I opened it to find a ring.

It was a silver heart surrounded by entwined hands.

"An Irish friendship ring," he said.

I like the Irish. Jack was gorgeously, redheadedly Irish. I was turning forty, and I was thinking that my luck with men was finally shifting. But the ring—although it wasn't cheap—looked inelegant to me.

I held my tongue and slipped it on, eyed it in the light.

"It's very nice," I said. "Thank you."

"Do you really like it?" he asked.

"Is it returnable?" I replied.

The next night was my party at the Chateau Marmont. Jack and some friends of mine were in charge. We invited a hundred guests, and filled the room with enough people to make it work pretty well. But by the end of the week I had grown weary of him—his morning chanting, his yoga, the elaborate washing of his face each night with organic oils and customized ointments. I called it his ritual ablutions. I thought he was a New Age narcissist, totally obsessed with his body. He thought I was unable to love, too judgmental, and crippled by my own cynicism. It broke my heart when he left me.

Since there's nobody else to step in and orchestrate my forty-fifth birthday tonight (my brother's away with his family), my friend Marisa has taken charge. I'm glad. We are in the town car she has ordered (my second today, thank you) and are headed up to a runway show at the Four Seasons. When we walk up the marble steps (she in very high-heeled Gucci boots and white leather jacket; me in a blue velvet suit that hangs a little funny), we are surprised to find that the show has already started. Fashion shows always start late. "What is going on here?" she says. "We're not that late!"

But there's nobody at the door out front to let us in. We stand outside a wall of tinted windows in an icy drizzle, peering in as models sashay past people we know. Marisa pounds on the glass, only to be ignored by a minxlike minion near the door.

How dare she keep us out?

"You know what," I say. "Why don't we go to the Grill Room and get drunk?"

"What time is it?" Marisa asks.

"Almost nine."

"Maybe just one. Silvano is expecting me for dinner."

"Really? Tonight?"

"I always join him at the restaurant at ten o'clock. You know that."

"Right. So you're ditching me?"

"You're welcome to come, Bob. Why don't you? I'm sure it'll be fine."

I thank her for trying to make my birthday work and apologize for making fun of her. But no, I don't want to intrude on her private dinner with her man. I kiss her good-bye, then go up to have a drink by myself in the bar upstairs, one of the most beautiful rooms in New York, dimly lit and hushed as a mausoleum.

"Expecting anybody?" the bartender asks.

I tell him no, order a Scotch, and sip it slowly. Then I tell myself that I'm fine.

And also a little too old for a midlife crisis.

## CHAPTER 7

# Hello, Eighty

Not long after my birthday, my brother and I realize
Dad's eightieth is coming up in late March. And it
occurs to us that even though it's only six months
after Mom's death, the old man will want us to plan him
a big party in Florida.

"I'd love it," he tells me over the phone. He thinks it
would be fun and the perfect way to reciprocate to all his
friends. "So many of them were so hospitable over the
years to your mother and me," he says.

Jewish tradition says no singing or dancing for a year
after a wife dies, and my mom was pretty devout. But
Dad's not. He lost any faith he had in God when Mom got
sick. Or maybe he just got tired of standing up and sitting
down at services. The kosher rules she liked to observe
got to be a drag, too. Bye-bye, latkes. Hello, lobster.

His is a God of fun, not discipline.

My mother's older sister, Aunt Phyllis, although fond of Dad, says she will not attend the party. "I just couldn't," she says. "It's too close. You understand." Mom's younger sister, Bev, who lives nearby in Palm Beach Gardens, eschews the event, too. "I just hope you aren't planning on having any dancing or singing," she says.

Actually, we are. For a sing-along. Because it just wouldn't be Dad if there weren't. I hire a pianist named Wes and book a room at the Hilton on the beach.

"We know it's what will make him happy, right?" I tell my brother.

"Yeah," he says. "But I just keep thinking about what Mom would say."

I do, and I don't. I know she didn't want to be a burden, she wanted us to enjoy ourselves. Nothing made her happier than to see all three of us happy. I guess that's why I took off for Scotland the week before she died in August 2002. I had been invited on a Scotch tasting tour, and, after a rough summer of one emergency after the next (alternating shifts with my brother and spelling for Dad, who could be counted on for only so much help with her medications and doctor's appointments), I felt ready for a break. I'm not sure why I didn't call home every day to see how she was doing in the hospital while I was away. She had fallen out of bed and injured her head. But when I left New York, it didn't seem all that serious, and my father and brother told me they wanted me to take my trip. In Scotland, we had a packed itinerary of distillery tastings and formal dinners, and with the time difference and lack of Internet service, it was hard to keep in touch with home. When I got to a phone a few days into my trip (a pay phone on a road beside hilly fields dotted with barley and sheep), Mom's voice was unrecognizable. She was babbling like a toddler. And I was so far away that I couldn't even touch her forehead or hold her hand. "I love you, Mom," I said into the receiver. "I'll be home soon. Get well, okay?" I hung up the phone and went back to my Scotch tour with a group of bickering New Yorkers. Like the Scotch we were tasting, there was a slightly bitter quality to the week, but it didn't occur to me to end it early. If anything, all the Scotch kept me oblivious.

One night toward the end of the tour, I was standing under a starry sky outside our hotel on Islay, a remote island known for its peaty Scotch. The northern lights— or something like them, anyway—were glowing on the horizon. Suddenly I was remembering the time as an adolescent I had woken my mother up in a motel room in Pennsylvania to take her outside to see the aurora borealis. While my brother and father slept, Mom and I stood together in our pajamas in a lonely parking lot, looking up at the shifting, spectral marvel. "You're the one in this family who sees the beauty in things, Bobby," she told me. And she was the one I could show the beauty to. Even at the end of her life, when she could barely walk, I could get her out of the house to walk down our street to enjoy a blazing sunset over the Great South Bay. She was willing to be inspired. And there was always so much I wanted her to see, so much I could show her. My father was too self-absorbed to listen, too busy with his own fun to be open to taking in the joy of anything I loved and wanted to share. But Mom, in her innocence, cared.

The Scotch tour continued. Why didn't I drop out and rush home to her? At the beginning of the last weekend I called in to my voice mail from a Glasgow hotel room.

A message. "This is your brother, Jeff. Remember me?

We haven't heard from you all week. I just thought you should know that Mom is in very bad shape in the hospital, and she may not be alive when you get back. I'm not sure why you haven't been in touch. Maybe you didn't want anything intruding on your holiday. All I know is that if you don't get your ass back here right away to show you're taking this seriously, then you will have so much to be sorry for that I imagine you'll be in therapy dealing with the guilt for the rest of your life." The click after his final words was as loud as a door slamming. I hung up the phone. My hands were shaking. Jeff could never do enough for Mom. He employed her once a week in his educational media business in Manhattan, giving her the sense of purpose she had lost when she retired from the library. He lavished her with gifts, monitored every doctor's visit, researched every new medication, hoping to find a way to fix things or at least make them better for her. Holiday dinners were always in one of his beautiful homes with his family. The devotion he could show my mother put me to shame. It never occurred to him to be anything but absolutely attentive. No matter what I would do for her, he'd do me one better. The result was that he raised the level of my own attentiveness, a very good thing. But now, here I was, so unhelpfully far away, and I couldn't reach him to explain my pointed absence.

I reached my father instead. He sounded circumspect. He told me not to worry, but that we had to pull together as a family. It was important my brother and I not fight. And it was important for Mom that we all love each other. I told him that I'd be home Sunday, and that if she slipped away without me, I had already said good-bye before I left. On a hot August Tuesday, after Scrabble, I had lifted her into her bed, gone into the living room, and played her piano, singing "Tumbalaika," an old Yiddish lullaby. And as I played, I heard her, straining to sing along in a ruined voice that was so different from the sweet one I knew from childhood. I finished the song, let the last chord fade, then went to her bed and kissed her good night, knowing I might not see her again.

"I already said my good-bye, Dad," I told him. "Jeff should know that."

Even over the phone thousands of miles away, I could sense his confusion. Like me, he wasn't one to be inconvenienced and had his own way of shrugging off heavy obligations. We were just so alike in that way, so starkly different from my brother.

"It's up to you if you want to come home, Bobby," my father said. "We all know Scotland is a long way away. And I can't make any promises, but I think she'll still be around on Sunday when you get back." I did leave Scotland early to be with her before she died. But only after spending another day there first, in Edinburgh, a city I had always wanted to see. I bought her a scarf, Merino wool in the pale blue color of her eyes.

She died a few days later, but was not coherent enough to say good-bye. Jeff told me it was the worst day of his life. For me, it was more complicated. Watching her take hours to expire in the hospital brought up feelings of both sadness and impatience. Her breath slowed as she lay without many tubes left to keep her going. But she was fighting to the end in a way that exhausted all of us. Finally, when the moment came and the life passed from her face, leaving it frozen, with mouth and eyes open, I felt horrified, then, callous as this sounds, liberated.

And now that she's gone, all I want is for Dad to stay healthy and happy, and not to be a worry. Six months have passed, and all those years of concern for her are behind us. She's gone. Dad is well, free to run around his beloved Palm Beach paradise unencumbered by responsibility. And even Jeff—who says he feels lost without Mom, and finds himself wanting to call her to tell her things when he knows full well that she isn't around anymore for him to phone—doesn't have the heart to sober him up.

So we decide to make a big celebration for the big eight-oh.

"Look, it's a hard call," Jeff says. "But it's what Dad wants, so let's do it."

I'm glad he's willing to err on the side of happiness. And I feel incredibly lucky not to be an only child.

Now it's the afternoon of the celebration, a sunny Saturday in March, when the weather in Palm Beach is its absolute best. Jeff is staying with his wife and kids at the Ritz-Carlton up the road. Under my tyrannical tutelage, Maddy and Ian, my niece and nephew, have worked up a number to perform, a parody of "Singin' in the Rain." I'm staying with Dad in his apartment, pasting photographs of him as a handsome young man with jet black hair and a gorgeous wife onto poster boards for a big display. My hands are sticky with rubber cement. I feel like a kid again, decorating the house to surprise him on a birthday. I still have to do the seating. But I also have to teach him the parody I wrote (the apple hasn't fallen far from the tree) for him to sing with me in front of his guests. His cell phone keeps ringing. CNN is broadcasting shrill, nonstop coverage of Bush's 2003 invasion of Iraq. I'm wildly opposed to it. Dad's all for it. His Republican politics annoy me. He's a disgrace to the Jews, a red state person in a blue state community. But, in a rare occurrence of self-mastery, I hold my tongue. It's the old man's eightieth birthday. And, really, what nicer way for him to celebrate than by singing in Palm Beach while there's bombing in Baghdad? I take my ukulele to the balcony, lure Dad outside.

"Okay, Dad, turn the cell phone off," I tell him. "We have to learn this song. Here's what I have. What do you think? It's to the tune of 'Bye Bye Blackbird.'"

I strum and sing:

*Wife is gone so sell the house,*
*Pack those bags, then fly south . . .*
*Bye bye winter!*

Dad is shaking his head as if he's just tasted something very unpleasant. Now he's getting up to walk away. I know I'm teasing him a little with the lyrics, but I can't help myself. I gently nudge him down. "Hey, where are you going, buster? We have to focus on this right now, or it'll be a mess at your party."

"I don't think so, Bobby," he says.

"What? What's the matter, Dad?"

"I don't want to sing that to my friends."

I don't blame him. It's all so confusing. Why are we both so lighthearted in the wake of Mom's death?

"Dad, I worked hard on these lyrics. Give it a chance."

"Don't you have anything else on offer?"

His cell phone rings again. He grabs it. I stand up over him. I want to grab it out of his hands, but I don't. Why am I so nervous? Is it because, despite all the lip service, this party is a bad idea, and I'm trying to make it his fault instead of mine? Or is it just that I like the opportunity to be in control of him? I don't want to embarrass myself singing unprepared in front of an audience, even if it's just family and friends.

"Can you turn your phone off until we learn this and you're showered and dressed, Dad?" He nods. I reach out and tousle his soft hair. "Please?"

I can't believe I am writing songs the way he did when he was in the army sixty years ago. And I can't believe how important it is *not* to bomb in Palm Beach tonight. It's absurd. After so many years of striving and failing to make my mark as some kind of professional performer, I'm giving my old man a hard time about the audience at his birthday party? And yet, I also know that, if we can just get a good song together as a father-and-son team, it'll make him proud and make his party very special.

"Bobby, maybe this isn't such a good idea. It's not worth the aggravation."

"But I wrote this song for you. I know how you love an audience."

"True, but don't you get a big kick out of doing this, too?"

"Me? Please! I am doing this in your honor, Dad! This is all for you!"

"If you say so."

I stare out at the intercoastal waterway, searching for composure. There are some pelicans gliding over the dock. They've always reminded me of my father, with their silvery heads and prominent straight noses, kind of clumsy looking, especially when they hobble, yet they glide so easily in the air, cruising along looking for nothing but some fish, a breeze, and a good time. Out there by the pool, an old man Dad knows is on a chaise lounge, tanning happily, so relaxed, without a care, it seems, without anybody nagging him to put on sunblock. *Wife is gone, rest in peace, move south, start over.*

"You know, if you really want to honor me, Bobby," Dad finally says, "you have to write something funny that my friends can relate to."

I take a deep breath. I let it out. Then I think of something.

"Okay, Dad. I have another verse. Try this, okay?"

I strum so hard it hurts my thumb.

*Pop all those blood pressure pills,*
*Medicare pays the bills,*
*Hello, eighty.*
*Doggy bags stocked in the fridge,*
*Early birds late for bridge,*
*Hello, eighty . . .*

"Okay, now this one has legs," he says.

"So sing with me, Dad, come on! The words are right here on this paper. I wrote them big for you." And much to my delight, he does, and in his finest croon.

*Can't complain life doesn't need improvement.*
*I just had a perfect bowel movement.*

"It's unpleasant but very true," he says, "I have to admit."

"Just sing, Dad, sing!"

*Cell phone stuck to my head,*
*Won't get off till I'm dead*
*Eighty, Hello!*

We end up coming up with something far tamer for the party, and pull up only a few minutes before it's to start. He hobbles with me across the Hilton parking lot in a blue blazer a little tight in front. The guests rolling in, a kind of march of senior soldiers, are in raw silk pastels, plus sizes, and sensible heels. One lady has jewelry in the same pale blue as her hair. Another has salmon nails that match her shoes and bag. Some are air-kissing each other as if they were allergic to lips. Mwah! The men are tan, white-haired, and slightly hunched, but with fiercely strong grips when they shake my hand. "Bobby! How are you? How's the writing coming? What's the news?"

I race to the bar for a vodka on the rocks. I need it. I'm completely ill at ease. This crowd, their questions, the memory of my mother hanging over us. Am I really going to get up in front of these people to sing?

My aunt Sylvia arrives in a deep green sweater dress and pearls, very dignified, as always. She's with Edie, in a navy blue pantsuit, classy and understated. As the new girlfriend, she doesn't know many people in this crowd. I know most of them.

They come at me like slow-moving bumblebees.

"Bobby, I haven't seen you in years!" says a Rhoda. "Bobby! You got gray! How old are you now?" Before I can answer, a Joanie takes my hand. Her hair is yellow as lemon Jell-O. "So handsome! So when are you getting married, Bobby?" she asks.

"Oh, Mrs. Lipshitz," I laugh, "I'm way too busy for that."

Thankfully, my brother comes over to stand at my side. Even though nobody is asking him awkward questions, he doesn't look all that relaxed in the middle of all this. Jeff and I have not made a habit of getting to know these people too well. I get another drink with him at the bar. I'm starting to feel buzzed as we scan this room full of faces from the past. It's like something between a fever dream and a Hadassah benefit. As is typical, we make little cracks as if we were still sarcastic teenagers.

"Look at the nose on that one," he says.

"I don't remember it being that size," I reply.

"Did she try to kiss you on the mouth?" he asks of a lady with too much lipstick.

"Full on," I say.

"You two are terrible," mutters Janet, my brother's wife.

It's true. We are terrible. And we still don't quite understand how such nice parents could have put such cynical sons on this earth. But here we are, two paunchy, graying, not particularly attractive brothers, amusing ourselves the way we have for years, at the expense of others. In a moment, I will stumble back through the crowd, glass in hand, and greet people warmly. I'll also tell the pianist I hired to pick up the pace between numbers. It's wonderful to see that all these people appreciate our dad so much. We stand back another moment to watch the happy unfolding of this spectacle we planned to make him happy. He looks thrilled. We're not displeased.

"Is that a toupee on Mr. Epstein?" I ask.

"Why don't you go ask him," Jeff says.

There are couples we recognize who loved both our parents. And there are others we don't know very well, many of them the tennis and bridge buddies my father ran to in mom's last years. And then, right in the middle of it, unashamed and natural as can be, Dad is standing with his arm around Edie as if she were our mother. I put my arm around Jeff, to steady myself at the sight.

"Well, he looks happy," he says.

"Hey, why not?" I say, as I suck down the rest of my drink and put the glass down on the bar. "Happiness is the goal here, right?"

"Right," he says. "Happiness is the goal."

The last time we had a big family party like this was their fiftieth wedding anniversary, just a year and a half ago at Sammy's Roumanian Steakhouse on the Lower East Side. It was a last-minute plan because Mom had become too weak to drive to the mountain resort my brother had booked. She could hardly get out of bed that day, let alone down the steps to the restaurant, where we'd gathered a small group. The traffic made everyone late. The food was cold. The music was way too loud, the band I hired not playing the klezmer music I had requested. But late in the evening, I looked up and saw them, dancing between tables, where there wasn't even a dance floor. Her arms were wrapped around his shoulders, his arms were wrapped around her waist. There was love in their eyes. They were dancing. And it was perfect.

Now my father is doing the same thing with Edie. Although there's no dance floor, he's moving her around while the pianist I hired plays "Begin the Beguine."

My brother turns to look away from the sight, and then heads off to make conversation with a cousin from Ohio. I'm a little overwhelmed, and also tipsy enough to wonder if I'm going to make it through the song Dad and

I still have to sing. I get a glass of water and step outside for some air. The sky is full of giant tropical clouds
in sorbet colors over the water. It's exactly the kind of
sunset my mother loved so much. I raise my glass to the
sky. "L'chaim, Mom," I whisper. "To life."

A few minutes later, Dad and I are finishing our song
to thunderous applause.

We hug each other.

"Happy birthday, young man," I say.

"I couldn't ask for more," he replies.

## CHAPTER 8

# Only the Lonely

It's a Friday night in May a couple months later. I am sitting in my chic and spare West Village apartment, staying in because I have no invitations to anything, and rationalizing that weekends are for amateurs in Manhattan. No dates, no parties. I've got my hotmail and glossy magazines to keep me busy—invitations and spam to delete and all those perfume ads to rip out and throw away—it can be very time-consuming, I find. With so many celebrity fragrances in your own living room, it's almost like they are right there with you. And when the magazines get tired, there's always TV. Plus, I still have to get to the gym.

I'm putting on my sneakers when my phone rings. Titillating. But it's only Dad. "Hi," I say. "Is everything okay?" He's back on Long Island for the summer. After selling the old house (with some help from his sons and a carting service) he has moved into a nice assisted-living facility in Great Neck. It's new and sunny and full of attractive people. So I'm pleased. Better zip code, better outfits.

"Have you made any friends, Dad?"

He's usually Mr. Happy Get-About. But there's a problem with the people he's seated with for his meals at this high-end facility, the Centra.

"They're vegetables," Dad says. "Not one of them can keep up a conversation."

To make matters worse, he had a fight with his regular bridge partner at the community center over his lateness for a game.

"I knew I was late, and I didn't care to be chastised," he says.

Nothing new. He would erupt at my mother every time she tried to suggest he had done something wrong; and if I ever make the mistake of criticizing him, it always ends badly. His mood goes from sunny to black faster than you can say "bipolar."

"So what are you going to do for bridge now?" I say, as I tie my sneakers while gripping the phone to my ear with my shoulder. "Got a new player in mind?"

"I've got some leads," he says. "But it won't happen overnight. I'm so desperate that I even called my partner to apologize, but she wasn't having it."

"Next time don't be so quick to pop off, Dad."

"I could just kick myself for behaving that way."

"Why don't you call a friend and go to a concert in that park you like so much?"

"The forecast is for rain tomorrow."

"How about a movie?"

"Nothing I want to see right now," he says.

"Hmmm," I'm yawning. "Aren't there any ball games on TV?"

I feel my head racing to come up with a suggestion that'll keep him happy. After half a dozen years of worrying about my mother, I've been enjoying not having to think much about him. But the darker tone of this call is disturbing. All winter in Palm Beach he was so good at amusing himself with Edie. I don't know why Long Island is more of a challenge. He's lived there most of his life. He has friends all over Nassau County, and was a longtime member of a tennis and bridge club not that far from Great Neck. But times change. Snowbirds eventually morph into more sedentary species, and stop the migratory pattern of coming back up north every year for their summers. Most of Dad's pals are living in Florida full-time now. He's a little at a loss.

"And what are your plans, Bobby?" he asks. "Do you have any?"

"Of course," I lie. "I'm fully booked this weekend. Why?"

"I was just thinking dinner would be nice tomorrow night," he says.

"I just told you I have plans."

"I know, and I don't expect you to change them."

"I need some advance notice, Dad. How about next weekend?"

"If that's what you can do, I'll take it," he says.

I have a pang of something. What is it? Remorse? Guilt? Half and half?

"Well, no, wait. Let me see if I can change things."

A few minutes later, after an interval long enough for me to pretend I've made some calls to rearrange my schedule, I call back to say I'm coming out tomorrow night.

"Oh, that's wonderful news," he says, "a dream come true."

Penn Station is the usual mob scene. Why are the slowest people blocking your way always the ones in sneakers and tracksuits? "Come on, people," I mutter as I weave through a crowd. "Move it!"

I make the train as the doors are closing, and spend the ride sweating and fuming at the inconvenience of this visit. Great Neck station is a half hour away. I step off and walk past flocks of young people heading into the city for Saturday night. Most of them are holding hands with dates, young, in love, or in what they think is love.

I cross the street and walk along Great Neck Road, under nice old trees, past purring luxury cars you'd never see where we used to live. It's only a block from the train to the Centra, a brand-new building with rococo pretensions and Marriott bones.

At the lower entrance, I sign a visitor's log under a security guard who is asleep, and step into the elevator. It ascends slowly and then stops on the main floor. A cross-looking white-haired woman in baby blue pantsuit thrusts her walker into the door. "That is not what I said," she's telling someone in the foyer. "I simply said it could be perceived as anti-Semitic, not that it *was* anti-Semitic! You should be more discerning." Done talking, she releases the elevator door to close. But it gets forced open again by an orange-haired woman wearing a sweatshirt with a sequined orange appliqué. She also takes her time stepping in. Then, finally, the doors close, and we are ascending. Nobody says thank you for waiting. "How are you?" lady one asks lady two. "You settling in okay?"

"Not great, not great. I miss my house. I miss the life I had."

"You'll get used to it. I did. But it takes some time."

The elevator stops on her floor. She takes her time getting out. Then it's the same thing on the next floor with the other one. Getting up to Dad takes forever.

Outside his door, on a small shelf, he has created a display: one tennis ball, photos of us and Mom. Inside, he has managed in very little time to re-create the multi-layered landfill of a mess that he had enjoyed at the old homestead.

He sold the old house so easily, without a moment's hesitation. Some children would find that difficult to take. Not me. Not my brother. We're happy to have it gone for good. His new apartment is nice. And it's filled with the furniture of my childhood. There's the oversize faux-Provincial lamp from our living room. There's the midcentury modern coffee table and the Chagall print from the dining room. So many memories from that old suburban house are all stuffed into this new apartment.

I sit on the same off-white couch where my brother and I sat on Mom's lap. The orange afghan she crocheted is draped over the back. You can never really leave the past behind, I guess, the aged gray poly trousers, for instance, that Dad is wearing tonight.

He looks sluggish. It could be the Lasix he's taking for blood pressure.

"So, Dad, how are you?" I say. "You ready to go out for dinner?"

"Oh, I don't know. Why don't we just order in?"

"But you asked me to come out here so you wouldn't have to dine out alone."

"Please. My hip hurts, and I'd rather stay off my feet."

This is not what I had in mind at all. This small apartment is no place for dinner. There isn't a surface that isn't occupied by statements from his myriad bank accounts, or magazine subscriptions, or carbon copies of his countless typewritten letters to friends and relatives. But I don't say anything. We order from a nearby Asian place, and Dad finds the shrimp fried rice delicious. His mood has been lightened by something simple, fresh, and unkosher. "Thank you for changing your plans so you could visit," he says.

"Sure," I say. "No big deal. But what's up? Why the long face?"

"Well," he says. "As you might know, Edie is in Philly for the summer."

"So you're having a little hiatus before next winter. Isn't that good for romance?"

"Not when she hasn't been returning any of my phone calls. All last week I was trying to reach her to let her know there's a bridge tournament coming up not far from where she lives. I thought I'd drive down. But she never called me back."

"Wow. Is she playing hard to get or something?"

"I wish it were so simple," he says. "But yesterday I finally got a letter from her. And it turns out that she has not one but two other old boyfriends in Philly."

"What? But she likes you. I saw her holding your hand in Florida."

"It's a nonexclusive arrangement, Bobby. And definitely restricted to Florida. I'm not welcome in her life up north, that much is clear."

"So, Dad, this attractive woman you were so pleased to have at your eightieth birthday party—and shuttle around as if she were the new love of your life—is jerking you around while she goes out with two other men in Philly? What's that about?"

"I wish I could tell you," he says. "But it was just a winter fling with us, I guess, like kids at summer camp." Then he sighs—Eeyore in a cardigan. "It's disappointing."

Okay, this is not good. He's not supposed to be worried about anything resembling romance yet.

After running his finger over the last morsels of his fried rice, he pulls a toothpick out of his shirt pocket and starts going at his molars while making sucking noises—a charming new habit. But, to lighten the mood, entertainment is on the way. He has taped a PBS Dinah Shore special.

"I hear she was a lesbian," I say.

"Don't be ridiculous," he says.

"No, seriously, there's a Dinah Shore golf classic in Palm Springs every year that's a big lesbian event. How do you explain that if she wasn't?"

"Foolishness," he says. "You don't have your facts straight. No pun intended."

He's not at all homophobic. But don't go messing with one of his icons. Dinah Shore, in her prime, was his ultimate goddess. The show he taped is a retrospective of her series from the 1960s, and it's called *Mwah* because that's the sound she made when she threw kisses. It's a mix of easy, breezy musical numbers suggesting that life is a bowl of cherries, or perhaps a can of fruit cocktail in heavy syrup. It's so upbeat and white bread—totally

Dad in its gestalt—that I find the kitsch quasi-compelling. How could anybody give off such relentless optimism? She knew how to blend with a man, too, show him off rather than outshine him. When she sings duets with Frank Sinatra and Bing Crosby, looking totally enamored in her pearls and impeccable poofy dresses, with bottle-blond hair so coiffed, I can't help but see my mother at her loveliest. She was a woman who knew how to let others shine, too. We watch the show together for an hour. The ease, the patter, the tuxedos and chiffon, it's all so soothing that it takes the edge off our night. Then it's over and time for me to go home. I put on my windbreaker.

"Why are you leaving?" Dad asks. "Spend the night! I've got an extra room."

I tell him that I can't and that I have to get home, even though I don't. I don't have anyone to go home to. I haven't had a date all spring.

"I could really use the company," he says.

Now I'm irked. First of all, the last thing I want is to wake up to him shuffling around in his pajamas in the morning, blowing his nose and pouring orange juice over his cornflakes. And the presumption is a little painful. I mean, why does he think that just because I don't have a wife and family that I'm at his beck and call, free to spend the night in this building of sclerotic seniors?

"I do have a life, Dad, you know."

"I know you do, Bobby."

"Just because I don't have a day job, family, two homes, and tennis habit, like some people we know, it doesn't mean that I don't have things to do with my life."

"So I guess my idea won't intrigue you."

"What's that?"

"Getting a house where we could live together."

"Huh? Where?"

"Somewhere that appeals to you, like the Hamptons."

"What's wrong with this place for you?"

"It's for old people," he says. "I'm not ready for this yet."

Living with my father, I know, is both a nice idea and a terrible one. Just imagining what the kitchen would look like makes me queasy. And when I'd have the occasional date, would he need to know about it? Would I be cooking for him? Washing his underwear? Of course, in an abstract sense, I admire all the cultures that revere elders enough to keep them close. Plenty of Americans take their parents into their homes, too, some for economic reasons, others because of compassion. When my mother's father was unable to live alone upstate in Utica in the 1980s, he moved to our Long Island house. He was a crusty old guy, a handball player and amateur boxer, who had a tendency to tease the cat and bend your ear with banalities. He was my only living grandparent, but—call me picky—not the kind I would have selected for myself had I been given a catalogue. He spent hours loitering at our kitchen table, tapping his fingers, with nothing to do but talk. I wasn't as nice as I could have been. But my father treated him with nothing but warmth and respect.

For a moment I envision my father and me living together in a house in the Hamptons—the sacred and elite area I can only visit as a renter or houseguest. But then I see him slurping his tea at breakfast and dumping salad dressing over our pasta at dinner. I see myself rushing past him to get to the phone before he answers it and proceeds to have inappropriate conversations with any one of my dates, friends, colleagues, or harried editors.

The fights, the odors, messes to clean up! Pills overhead and underfoot. Never!

"Thanks, but I don't think so, Dad. I'll live my own life, if you don't mind."

It sounds harsh. But neither of us has ever been much good at protecting the other from our feelings. So why can't I just tell him that I want to go home, back to the city, right now? Instead, I take a deep breath and sit back down, and we play Scrabble. He wins. Then, while I scoot around trying to clean up the monumental mess he has made of his apartment, he turns on a ball game. I have been trying to teach myself not to feel so anxious around him. But I can't help it. I'm just so bored here, and for a moment I find myself dreading all the relentless years— plodding, dutiful, strained—of this ahead of me. I don't want to be here another minute. It's ten P.M. I've done my time. But just as I'm about to say good night for real, he pulls out a copy of *Jewish Week* and thrusts it at me. It's opened to the Personals page.

"Before you go," he says, "there's something I want to ask you."

"Okay. What? I have to catch a train. Speak!"

"I wonder if you wouldn't mind calling the ads I've circled here."

He places the newspaper in my hands. It is stained with tea.

"What? I don't understand."

"I would do it myself, but it says here that you need a landline to get through to the 900 number that's listed, and I only have a cell phone."

"You're kidding, right?"

"It's two dollars a minute, but I'll reimburse you."

"I don't get it, Dad. You're not making any sense."

"You're such a contemporary person," he says. "You know the dating scene."

"I know it's a nightmare, that's all I know."

"I thought you could show me the ropes a little, get me started."

"But, Dad, does it occur to you that these ads are called Personals for a reason? This is absolutely none of my business."

"Okay," he says, as he takes the newspaper away from me. "Just thought I'd ask."

I stare at him a moment. He looks so anxious, so needy, as if he'd just been let down by the only person with the keys to the kingdom. I take off my jacket, throw it down on the couch, and sit back down. This cannot be happening. I grab the newspaper.

"Okay. All righty. I see you've circled some here."

"Two in particular are alluring."

With a little derision, I read aloud in a thick New York accent: "'Attractive, youthful widow, slim and petite, incurable romantic, seeks active kindred soul, seventy to eighty, to share life's joys and whatever. Should be refined, intelligent, interesting, and secure.'

"'Whatever,' Dad? What's that about?"

"Who knows, Bobby."

"Dad, she says she's looking for refined. Is that you?"

He shrugs and says, "I can be refined when I have to be."

"Okay, you circled this one, too," I say, moving on. "Let's see what it says: 'I most definitely do not snore! Amusing Jewish lady seeking nice Jewish lad fifty-seven to sixty-eight . . .' Dad, last I checked you were eighty."

"People mistake me for seventy all the time. And I wouldn't mind a younger gal."

I hand the newspaper back to him and stand up.

"Come on! Mom died, what, seven months ago? Okay, so you're not into mourning. But are you so incapable of being alone for a year? Look at me, I'm always alone, and I'm not lonely. I have lots of friends, and so do you. What is this desperate need you have to be in love?"

He shakes his head. "I don't know," he says. "It just worked so beautifully with your mother for fifty years that I'd love to do it again."

*Do it again?* I'm thinking. *Do it again?* First of all, he's old. Hasn't he had enough? Second, was it really so great? Mom used to call herself a tennis widow and him a married bachelor. He was late for his own wedding because of a tennis game, and when he showed up he had forgotten his shoes. He was a barely manageable husband who poured low-cal maple syrup over Mom's labor-of-love noodle pudding and drove her around in a car that smelled from dirty socks and a long forgotten fish sandwich. He was moody, tardy, impossibly willful, and prone to explosions when crossed. "Damnit, Ethel" was his trademark eruption. It could be over the littlest thing—a wrong turn on the highway, a botched volley at net, a decision she made without him.

Of course there were times when he had reason to feel frustrated. She was a timid driver, just as she was timid in life, a woman who would cancel all plans if the rain was coming down too hard. That's why she was so often telling him no. On vacations he'd want to look up people they hardly knew, take leftover food off plates from empty restaurant tables, and start sing-alongs at big parties where he didn't even know the hosts. She couldn't help being the naysayer in the relationship. But the thing is, he'd do whatever he wanted anyway, so why aggravate him by being negative? She put her foot down hard enough to make a difference only once, early on in their marriage, when he came in after midnight from a card game and found her in tears. He never did it again. He cared too much to upset her. Yes, he could have been around more for her when she was sick. But good-time Joe could take only so much of her infirmity. Well, maybe that was her fault for insisting she didn't want a health-care aide as much as we begged her to hire one. Her thrift made things hard for all of us in her last years. His didn't help either. "I'll be back before supper" is all he'd say as he left her alone in the house.

But *then* I think of the times he made her happy even at the end, shuttling her to concerts and parties with old friends and bringing her chocolate cake from the diner where he stopped after bridge. She loved the sweets he'd bring her, the cheesecakes and milk shakes she needed to keep her weight up, even as my brother and I nagged him to make sure she was eating greens and healthy foods, too. And there were all those times he made her laugh with his absurdly obscene jokes.

And there was the singing. Often, as a kid, I'd look out my bedroom window and see them in the backyard, singing love songs to each other. They weren't therapized people. They weren't the cosmopolitan or mod parents of their era, having key parties and chardonnay spritzers in modern glass homes. They didn't have the language or the big ideas. But they had their songs, and two unusually lovely voices that wrapped around each other with the ease of wisteria branches. Sometimes I'd sneak down the stairs in my pajamas and spy on them dancing to cha-cha records in the den and laughing into the night. They weren't stylish, but they were beautiful dancers. Dad was smooth enough on his feet to make Mom seem like a natural. "One, two, cha-cha-cha," I'd hear her count carefully. And around she'd go, one hand in his, one held up in the air for balance. Whatever skill they lacked they made up with their joy. They were so happy, long after couples got bored with each other and took each other for granted. That was, I suppose, the benefit of a marriage with my father, an unpredictable man with a kind heart who insisted on romance. I was both attracted and repelled, watching the kick they got out of each other. Would I ever have that? Did I even want it, let alone need it? They were just so buoyant on those late nights in the house, floating in their suburban bubble, so young, so in love. More in love than I imagined, or perhaps feared I would ever be.

So how can he just go dismissing all of it now—all of that—after fifty years of marriage? Who knows? But the old man seems to need a mate again, and I guess, now that Mom is gone, the only question at hand is, Who would love a poorly dressed, irascible, but sweet and well-meaning suburban Republican like him? I don't know. But I guess I should try to help him out. Because if he's happy, then I don't have to worry about his being lonely, and then *I* can have some peace and be left alone to my life.

It's almost eleven P.M. The trains back to the city are running only once an hour from Great Neck station now. There's one in ten minutes. I bolt up from his couch.

"Okay, Dad, I'm going home. I'm sorry if you're a little

lonely. Give me those Personals. I'll make those calls if I have time."

"That would be terrific, Bobby," he says as he walks me to his door, where he tries to give me a big hug, but I dodge it and end up patting him on the shoulder instead.

"Oh, and do me a favor, Bobby," he says. "When you give women my cell phone number, make sure you tell them to call me after nine P.M. Off-peak minutes."

"Sure, Dad, why not?" Then, when I'm closing his door behind me, he calls out: "Don't you feel a little impish doing this?"

Pimpish is more like it.

## CHAPTER 9

# Outdated

Appalled as I am with Dad and his Personals page, he's right. I am familiar—unhappily familiar—with the dating scene. Most of those I meet on my online dating site can't even be bothered to reply to my e-mails. But then, I ignore my share, too.

Never mind the lure of romance, never mind the high of new love. These days, dating is nothing but a sport of procure, dodge, and discard. You have to know how to traffic lightly in disappointment. You have to be able to be both deft and cruel. It has become a kind of social warfare, and for my demographic of baby boomers, the comic narrative of our time. The worse the date is, the better the story value for later.

The weekend after Dad has thrust his personal ads at me, I end up with three dates in one night. Bumper crop

on a nice evening in May. I am meeting date number one
for a drink at the trendy Bottino in Chelsea. I rush in
late. He's looking at his watch, grim. And cute. Very cute.
Soft honey brown hair that I loved in his online profile.
And he is better built than I envisioned. Love the blue
eyes and white button-down shirt. He doesn't dress to
draw attention to himself, like I do. He knows he doesn't
have to.

"Hi! So sorry I'm late! Been waiting long?"

"Fifteen minutes," he says.

"I'm so sorry. I'm Bob."

"John."

We shake hands. I like him immediately. But even
after a drink, I can't tell if he likes me (later I find out—
because I never hear from him again). But hey, no time
to dwell tonight. After a half hour I have to say good-bye
so I can get uptown to date number two, a setup who is
supposed to look like Pete Sampras. And he does. But not
in a good way. I down a double Scotch. I'm free to behave
poorly now. "Don't you just love Madison Avenue?" I
spout as we pass terriers on leashes and trophy wives
on diet pills. "I just find the people are so much better
looking up here!" In Central Park, a line of cherry trees
is blossoming so extravagantly that I shriek like a girl,
"Better than the couture shows in Paris!" Then I have a
sneezing fit that leaves me red-eyed, runny-nosed, and
spewing obscenities at the trees, as if it were their fault
for being in bloom.

A half hour later it's dinnertime, and I stumble back
downtown (heart palpitating from my cocktail of Scotch
and Sudafed) to meet bachelor number three. He looks
promising there at the sushi bar. Love the rust-colored

hair. I walk up to him with real hope in my heart. But wait a minute. I'm not sure, but I think I see love handles beneath that sweater. Just because *I* have them doesn't mean anyone else can. No chemistry, no interest. In less than an hour, the date is over, and I'm out the door with nothing to show for all my trouble tonight.

It was just another night that yielded nothing but lower back pain, indigestion, a little pang of loneliness, and then, eventually, as I stomp home with the overly purposeful footsteps of a man who's had too much to drink, a renewed commitment to being a thriving single person in the most sophisticated city in the world. Of course, it was a little easier being a thriving single person when all my friends were single, too. Now that so many of them are getting hitched and having children, I don't have as many playmates as I used to. People I know are actually finding meaning and love in their lives.

"How was the date?" Marisa asks later that night.

"You mean dates," I say. "I don't know why I bother."

"Yes, you do, Bob. You want to be in love, don't you?"

She doesn't wait for my reply. Her husband is calling on her other line.

## CHAPTER 10

# Bird in a Guilty Cage

I wake up the next morning to a ringing phone. I have a hangover. By the third date last night I was on my fifth drink, and now I'm paying for it. The sun is too bright in my apartment. It's eleven A.M. "Hi, Bob!" It's Dad. "Just wondering what time to expect you." Shit. I feel like crap, don't want to get on the train to Great Neck today. But it's been a couple weeks, and I owe him a visit. Add guilt to hangover and stir.

"Dad. Hi. How are you?"

"Could be worse. Keeping pretty busy."

"Good. Did you find a new bridge partner?"

"Not yet. But I had a decent game the other day over at the town pool with a woman from California. Unfortunately, she went home today."

I chug some orange juice from a carton, pop three as-
pirin, put on some coffee, look out the window, and see
it's pouring. No, I don't want to go see him today.

"And how are you settling in there? How is the world
of assisted living?"

"Not great. I still have these terrible, incommunicative
people at my dinner table. They sit in silence for entire
meals, and I can't get a conversation going."

That's odd, I think, because getting conversation going
is usually his specialty.

"I'm so discouraged," he's saying, "that I'm eating upstairs in my apartment."

This is exactly the kind of whiny call I'd make to him
and my mother for the first thirty years of my life, when
things weren't working out as I had expected. So I should
be more attentive now. But I'm bored with this residen-
tial-living drama of his, just as I'm bored with his inabil-
ity to settle in and enjoy Great Neck, which is a paradise
for senior citizens—full of activities for them. I turn on
the TV. It's a *Golden Girls* rerun. Those women had it
figured out, living together so they weren't isolated, but
still playing the field so they weren't out of the game. But
that's TV, not real life.

"Maybe you could switch to another table, Dad. Do you
want me to call the executive director there?"

"Please, no! Just stay out of it!"

"Don't raise your voice at me. I'm just trying to be helpful."

There is, of course, nothing I'd rather do than stay out
of it. But for what the place is charging, there's no reason
he should be miserable for three meals a day. The whole
point is that the Centra is *not* supposed to be like a nurs-

ing home. I thought it was supposed to separate the in-
valids at meals from the ones like Dad who still have all
their marbles. Other assisted-living facilities keep the in-
valids on a separate floor. It pisses me off. I was thinking
he'd just settle in there, get with the Great Neck groove,
and I wouldn't have to worry about him at all. I need him
not to need me.

"So what else, Dad? Nothing nice to report?"

"I went to the movies the other night."

"So you don't mind going to the movies alone? Me neither. It's easy, right?"

"Who says I went alone? I went with a lady named
Honey."

"A lady named Honey?"

"She's an administrator in my building, widowed,
younger than me."

As he tells me the story of her life in some detail, I
can't help thinking about the time he met another Honey,
a New York drag performer. I was reporting on the opening of a Broadway show ten years ago. Dad was my date. It
was an evening full of high spirits and higher hair. During
intermission I looked up to see him across the aisle in
an animated conversation with a vision in a shimmering
gown, flawless wig, and powerful makeup—my father's
idea of ultimate ladylike glamour. He had no idea he was
talking to a man, not a socialite. But here's the thing I'll
never forget about that night: Lady Honey (or was it Lyp-
sinka, another drag star?) looked entranced with him as
he talked. Everyone—men, women, and those who are in
between—finds my father charming.

So I shouldn't be surprised that a lady named Honey
has hopped into his scene the minute Edie in Florida

hopped out. I am trying to get a picture of her in my mind. He says she's petite. Short blond hair. Perky. Okay, but would she be an attractive addition to our lives? And is she capable of making Dad happy so I won't have to worry about him anymore? "So, a movie date," I say. "With benefits?"

"That was my plan, but not hers."

I had been making a joke. Now I don't want to hear any more. Not about how he thought about inviting her up to his apartment after the movie, but could not because then someone in the building might see them together. I also don't want to hear about how he was angling to get invited over to her place, but with her daughter there it wasn't "conducive." And I certainly don't want to hear how he wanted to do a lot more than hold hands with her in the car while parked in her driveway. He tells me anyway. "But she wasn't showing any interest at all," he says. "And I was getting so frustrated that I finally just told her we had no future."

Hearing this, this lady named Honey became distressed, then agitated.

"But, Joey, I have feelings for you, and I thought you had them for me," she said.

He told her that it was never his plan to get serious, and that she was making too much of his intentions. "And frankly, I was hoping for something more physical with you from the start," he said. "But I guess that's not in the cards." She didn't know what to say. Awkwardness ensued in his Avalon. The porch light was on at her Tudor house off Great Neck Road. He turned on some easy listening for a more soothing and romantic ambience. He tried to take her hand. She pulled it away. Frank Sinatra was singing "Strangers in the Night" on the radio. He waited it out a few minutes, thinking she'd succumb. Then he couldn't wait anymore. Nature was suddenly calling, and since she wouldn't invite him in, he had to bum-rush her out of his car.

"Side effect of the Lasix," he said. "Gotta go! Sorry!"

She slammed the door and disappeared into her house.

"She's too high-strung," he tells me. "Kind of like a Chihuahua."

So why go out with her? Why get involved at all? Because she offered to treat? He never says no to anyone. He likes to complicate life, not simplify it.

"So now, what time can I expect you today?"

My foot suddenly starts tapping. I tell him I've got a cold.

"Oh. That's a shame. I was hoping to go for a ride."

Silence for a second, a void I can't cross. He's probably waiting for me to change my mind. I don't want to be one of those kids who has contact with his parents only by phone. On the other hand I could never be the son who calls every day and visits every weekend. Technically, I guess I could. I do have the time. But I just don't have the patience. What he has to offer isn't fun. I wish I knew how to make it fun.

"Let's try for next weekend, okay, Dad?"

"Sure. But, before we say good-bye, I want to ask you something."

"What's that?"

"Did you ever call the ladies in those personal ads I showed you?"

I had completely forgotten about it.

"Sorry. I haven't gotten around to it. Is it really so hard? Don't you think you can just meet someone at one of your bridge games?"

"Bridge women are so difficult. The ones I'm meeting in Great Neck are especially demanding and spoiled. Mom was the opposite."

"Right. She *never* got her way. What about the women in your building?"

"Not for me. I can tell."

"What are you looking for anyway?"

"I just need someone with a good figure who doesn't smoke. Preferably Jewish. Republican a plus. I'm going to hold you to your promise to make those calls for me."

We say good-bye, and I hang up the phone. What is going on here? Am I really going to be pimping for my father? A few minutes later I dig out the Personals page with the ads he circled and place it at distance from me at my desk, like something unappetizing. Tripe, perhaps. Or liver. Then I take a deep breath and pick up the phone and dial the first number he's circled. My heart pounds, brain races. A machine picks up, and I get a recorded voice that sounds like a honking horn.

"Hello! This is Shelly Shapiro. I'm *saw-ry* I can't take your *cawl*, but please leave your name and *numbah* twice, and I'll get back to you. Have a *mah-velous* day."

*Beep!* I hang up without leaving a message. I can't stand that accent. My mother wasn't a sophisticate, but she grew up upstate and had no accent. My dad doesn't have one either. I'm not used to harsh voices in my family and don't want any now. I look at the other ad he circled, call the number, and get another machine.

"Hi, it's Seal, let's make a deal, leave me a message, don't be a shlemiel."

Absolutely not! I hang up. What kind of women did he pick?

My imagination starts projecting a borscht-belt lineup of unpalatable ladies, anxiously waiting in the wings to step out and make a mess of his new life.

I look at other listings on the page: *Attractive Youthful Widow! Fine Leading Lady! Outgoing Brooklyn Beauty! Sabbath Observing Honey! Classy Energetic Yenta! Compassionate Pianist! Don't Passover Me! Eat My Kugel and Go Straight to Heaven!* They're all pretty much alike, stipulating callers be "secure" and "a gentleman." I guess that means they have to have money and manners. Wait. Here's a decent listing that's also geographically suitable. It's for a Roz from Roslyn. College-educated. Slim. Lively. She sounds okay. So I call her, find that the voice on her answering machine sounds acceptable, and leave her a message. Then I leave one for a Minna from Manhasset—very good zip code right next door to Great Neck—who sounds okay, too.

I put down the Personals page and the phone and find that I'm smiling deviously.

And thus begins my father's year of dating dangerously.

# PART II

# The Comedy of Eros

## CHAPTER 1

# Geriatrix (cont.)

Botox, lipo, cardio, angioplasty. Seventy is the new forty, right? Add to that the boost that dating gets when seniors have cell phones and Internet access, not to mention physical trainers and Viagra, and you get the turbocharged arena my dad's about to enter. Three women for every man! And just because these men are old doesn't mean they're nice. How else would you explain the rash of codgers who divorce their first wives for women half their age? Hard as it is to believe, it was always women whose sex drives were actually stronger than men's in their later years. Now things have changed. In Scottsdale, Arizona, a cyclotron of senior society, one man observed in a newspaper article that the women he knows "wouldn't trade their cat for a man" and added that they aren't looking to get involved "with some randy eighty-year-old," at least not on a full-time, intimate basis. Still, with demographics weighted so heavily in favor of men, and with plenty of highly focused women anxious to remarry for their own reasons (money, or the convenience of someone to have on their arm), even a shlump who was not much of a ladies' man in high school can be a total catch in his senior years for no other reason than he is still alive and drives at night.

"Some of the women are total carnivores," says my aunt Sylvia, who lost my delightful uncle Dan twenty years ago, and has been happily widowed and entirely consumed with her family and her Palm Beach and Vermont lives ever since. "My cousin Raymond is eighty years old. The woman circle around him like vultures. He's a nice-looking man and a good sport who likes a good time, so he's always with another one. When he ended the last relationship—this was with a woman ninety years old, mind you—she passed away a few months later and all her friends said she died of a broken heart. Can you imagine? The whole thing is so ridiculous. Your father has a million things to keep him busy, but he still has to meet someone to love. It's just so funny."

I wish I could have more of a sense of humor about the whole thing.

But it's just too uncomfortable, so I decide to get a column out of it. Enough people my age are going through something similar. I interview a man who owns New York's oldest dating service. He tells me that children who come to his office to set up their elderly fathers request women of a similar age to their mothers. Then, the fathers call the service (without their children knowing) and declare that they want young, not old. So the father finds a match, and the kids get jealous, and, of course, issues of inheritance come into play when marriage comes up as a possibility. It's all perilous. "But you just have to pull yourself back," this dating maven tells me, "and let your dad do his thing and pick who he wants."

Aunt Sylvia agrees. "You father is his own man, and he needs to meet someone nice and understanding," she counsels. "But I don't know if he's going to meet who *you* want him to meet." I tell her he'd better or I'm going to make myself scarce in his life.

"My goodness," she says. "If you had kids dating, you would be impossible!"

That's exactly what this feels like. I'm playing father to a son, a kid!

"Because," says a woman I call who wrote a book about second wives, "when he's on a date, he feels young again, as if he's starting a second life. And so does the woman. There's just all this potential ahead of them, a whole new future."

"Potential for trouble," I say. "Potential for total disruption."

"Potential for love and a new life," she corrects me.

I take a few notes for my column and thank her for her time.

"Wait a minute," she says. "You know? I think I have someone for him, a friend of my mom's. She plays bridge and winters in Palm Beach, just like your dad."

"But where does she live up north?"

"She has a place on Fifth Avenue and a condo in Sun Valley, I think."

Fifth Avenue? Sun Valley? Whoa! I'd love that. But is all this too rich for him? This lady sounds very haute couture, and my dad's so wash-and-wear. I pooh-pooh it.

"I just think he's way too down-market for a woman like that," I say. "He isn't worldly or cultured. He doesn't even read the *New York Times* unless a neighbor drops it off. He won't be up to the standards of someone so fancy."

"Come on, Bob, what kind of attitude is that?"

"Defensive pessimism. It won't work."

"Maybe it will, maybe it won't," this woman says. "But I'm going to call my mother right now and get a number. Her name's Florence. And, Bob, don't ever say he isn't good enough for anyone. He's your dad. And you love him, don't you?"

## CHAPTER 2

# Date Date Goose

t's a drizzly May evening. An ash blonde with no body fat named Ann is waiting outside her high-end condominium in one of Long Island's Gold Coast towns. She is worried about the humidity and her hair. She just had a wash and set and hopes this weather doesn't frizz it up too much. She reminds herself not to order ice cream for dessert because she left her Lactaid upstairs. Her heart is beating a little fast, it seems. She's nervous. Scaring up a date isn't easy for a woman her age, and this Joe Morris sounded so pleasant on the phone. His voice was smooth, his demeanor breezy. Geographically suitable, Jewish, a retired judge with two sons who have Ivy League degrees. What would he look like? She was picturing if not a Jewish Robert Goulet, then someone Alan King–like, may he rest in peace. "Tonight, tonight, won't be just any night," this Joe Morris had crooned to her on the phone earlier. It wasn't her favorite song or musical (she prefers classical music to show tunes and instrumental to vocal), and certainly it wasn't her idea of suave, but his enthusiasm and spirit were encouraging.

Maybe he could get her to lighten up. That might not be a bad thing.

After waiting fifteen minutes in front of her building, she sees a silver sedan pulls up. It's no knight in shining armor. If she's expecting him to get out of the car and open the door for her (call her old-fashioned, she still thinks it's a nice gesture), she soon realizes it isn't happening and opens the door for herself and says hello. She gets in. Behind the wheel there's a man who looks good for eighty—nice head of hair, young face—but is still eighty.

Her husband had been eighty when he got sick. For three years she was his nursemaid, companion, and link to the world. Her children were not around. They live on the West Coast so they could only visit every few months. Friends stopped calling. They had their own problems. She didn't keep up with them either. It was enough to keep the house and his medications in order, not to mention all the doctors and hospital visits, a full-time job, like taking care of a baby, only this time there would be no future in it, nothing hopeful. And as her husband's mind and body drifted further and further out, she felt as if she were at sea with him, and each new medical trouble felt like another rogue wave tipping her boat just as it had barely righted itself from the last. He died last year. They were married fifty-five years. She's still not over it. But now she's in a stranger's car on this—and there is no other word for it—date.

"I thought we could have Chinese," he is saying.

"I had Chinese last night," she replies. "How about Japanese?"

"I don't care for Japanese," he says. "What about Italian?"

Italian is fattening, and she's on a low-carb diet, but she doesn't want to get into it now. Too early for conflict. She's aware of the fact that she's not the easiest person. Her kids tell her that all the time. She wonders if that's why they've chosen to live so far away. She does wish she could be less specific in her demands. But she knows what she likes, and why is that so wrong? Men that way are considered decisive. Women are considered picky and difficult. It doesn't win points on a first date to be particular.

*Why not try to just go with the flow, Ann?* she tells herself.

Because he has the air-conditioning on high in his car, that's why, and it's not just freezing her arms, it's blowing her hair to kingdom come.

"Would you mind turning it off?" she asks.

"I like it on high," he says. "For my allergies."

"I prefer to ride without it" is all she can say.

He turns it down to medium. "How's that? Better?"

Barely. And not her idea of accommodating at all. And why would he have the ball game on the radio? And why is he going on about the Mets when he hasn't even asked if she's interested in baseball? What kind of conversation is that for the first few minutes of a first date? Her only response is to clam up. Well, she's never been a bubbly person. But a particularly dark mood starts coming over her now, before they even get out of the car, which is a mess, and smells rank. At a stoplight at Little Neck Road, when he changes topics from the Mets to bridge, she wonders about the gurgling in her stomach. Is it the reflux? Did she take her Nexium? Is she going to make it through this dinner date without having to keep running to the powder room?

And then she wonders what she's doing here anyway. She doesn't want another man. But without one her social life is so barren. Articles she's been reading in the AARP magazine and Long Island *Newsday* keep suggesting that widows are far more self-sufficient than widowers. But her friends are all in couples. It's awkward, always needing a bridge partner, being the single person at the dinner party. Her kids worry that she's lonely. She tells them she isn't. But in some ways she is. So she tries her luck and puts in a listing and gets this Joe Morris. A total stranger. As he pulls off Northern Boulevard to the restaurant—Villa something or other; not one she'd heard anything good about—she wonders if she should just say she's not feeling well and have him take her home. Dinner ahead looms longer than a High Holiday service.

She endures. As does my father. But just barely, I find out later.

"She was a total dud," he tells me. "I could have kicked myself for following through with her. From the moment we spoke on the phone, I could tell she wasn't right for me. She sounded so morose about her husband's death. And it's a cardinal rule of dating that you don't talk about your ex right away, whether deceased or divorced."

I understand. But I also sympathize with her. I mean, I know I'm never my best self on dates. And besides, how do you erase the imprint of decades of marriage?

"She got in the car and immediately started hocking me about the air-conditioning," he says. "I knew I had a problem personality on my hands."

So he discards her, like an old plum. And there's not even a moment to sympathize with the poor woman, or give her a second chance, not with all the options he has to choose from. In fact, the moment I threw out the bait for him by responding to those Personals ads, he's gotten very busy, pulling in one thing after another flapping on his hook. Man-eaters. Bottom-feeders. Gefilte fish.

Here's the short list:

Rita is a disappointment to him because she doesn't smile enough. "She's no Dinah Shore," he says. "If I can't get a smile out of her, there's no point in moving forward." Selma, who is a little plump for his taste, wants to talk about the *Kama Sutra* and get him to take a workshop in the Poconos. "Attractive but a nut, a Jewish Shirley Mac-Laine," he says. Lorna used to be a socialist. "When she told me that, I asked for the check and sent her home." He does like Shirley, whom I selected for him based on her upright Personals ad and good Manhattan address. But when he tells me she has a rent-controlled studio apartment and has to work two bookkeeping jobs to support herself (at her advanced age?) I don't like it at all. That must mean she isn't very well off. That's no good. Then he cheerfully tells me that her ex-husband had psychiatric problems and that one of her kids is obese and a gun hobbyist. Can you imagine what a Thanksgiving dinner with them would be like? I'm appalled. But Dad just finds her pleasant and pretty. "She's coming out to Great Neck for a second date this week," he says. "And I'd like you to meet her." I tell him I don't meet anyone until after the fifth date. After their third, he's put off when she mocks him for taking cell phone calls over dinner. That's the end of that. He laments to me on the phone each night, telling me he's never going to meet anyone as nice as my mother. I wish he'd go for Roz, whom I found on his Personals page, and actually think is a pretty good package. Roz is from Roslyn and has a degree from Cornell. Roz is slender, according to her profile, easygoing, Jewish-minded, and financially secure. Plus, her son is a doctor. I want my father to go with the lady with the son the doctor! Is that so wrong?

"Yes, she's better educated, Bobby," he says. "But I don't think we'd mesh."

"Based on one conversation? What could be so bad?"

"She kept interrupting me, and finishing my sentences. Very hard to take."

"Oh, come on, Dad. That's no big deal. You do that to me all the time. Why not give her one more try?"

"Because I don't want to."

"Yes, you do."

"No, I don't."

Oh, my God. What am I doing? What is *he* doing? You hear about helicopter parents who hover over every aspect of the lives of their children. Am I becoming a helicopter son? I'm calling him more often now. And paying more attention when he calls. What can I say? I'm dying to know what the story is with this date and that one. Gone are his blathering soliloquies about the rerun he saw on TV. In are the episodic sagas of microwave relationships that heat up and cool off in a second—Senior *Sex and the City*. Or maybe it's *Desperate House Widows*. There was the nice lady who left him in the parking lot of the Nassau

County Museum of Art after he scolded her for lighting a cigarette. The buxom yenta still so upset about her divorce that she cried on their first date. A former Rockette who drank too much. A retired Gestalt psychiatrist who wanted him to be more forthcoming with his feelings. Lines of them, like planes overhead, waiting to land at LaGuardia. May, Ray, Fay—Fran, Ann, Nan—Bunny, Honey, Sunny. His reports are so volatile, so unexpected, so hilariously bizarre that they make dating tales of my friends seem banal. Too bad all his efforts lead to nothing. Dates fizzle before they even start. His is nothing if not a flitty dating scene.

But then, so is mine. A Scott e-mails in late May. He saw my profile online. I'm thrilled. His profile is witty. He's red-haired and ruddy. Beefy but not fat. Outdoorsy yet well read. Rugged yet urbane. He's *perfect*! In the city he lives on a houseboat off Seventy-ninth Street. He has a country place in Vermont and a tractor. We meet for a first drink and have a great time. He goes off to the country for two weeks. My spirits are high for his return. This could finally be the one. We agree on Saturday night for a second date. He e-mails that he'll call to tell me when and where. He never does. I sit in my apartment, heart leaping like a jilted senior on prom weekend each time the phone rings. I'm devastated. Then I get over it. It's not the first time it's happened. And you know what? I'm fine on my own. I'm resigned to sleeping alone. I get my eight hours a night better that way. Nobody to disturb my sleep or be bothered by my snoring.

I tell myself this often and believe it. Or believe that I'm believing it anyway.

But my dad is another story. He believes that the only way to live life is in love, and he won't rest in his quest.

So now I find myself pimping for him wherever I go. If an upstairs neighbor has a widowed mother with a nice figure in Queens, I get her number and pass it on to him. If I meet someone at a party with an aunt who is college-educated and plays duplicate bridge, I make sure Dad knows, and takes it seriously.

Maybe love at his age isn't as hopeless as we think it is.

"It's a little like being a teenager all over again, with nothing but the future ahead," he says. "Do you know that the other night I had to pick up a date and introduce myself to her daughter? She was looking me over at the front door as if I were a juvenile delinquent. I told her that I'd have her mother in by eleven P.M. and not to worry."

"Like you were taking a date to the prom, Dad? So did you score?"

"She was a very appetizing woman, but her politics were such a turnoff that I couldn't kiss her on the lips good night."

"So you didn't get any nookie?"

"Bubkes."

It's a sunny May afternoon, and we are pulling up to Stepping Stone Park in Great Neck. Gardens, fountains, and lawn rolling down to Long Island Sound. The bench he heads for is the closest to the parking lot because his hip won't take him farther.

"Dad, you know that walking is good for your circulation, don't you?"

"Please, Bobby, don't pressure me," he says, as he lowers himself onto the bench, with a moan and a sigh. "This is fine. We can sit right here and watch the world go by."

Out of the corner of my eye I see someone, a woman of a certain age, holding the *New York Times*. She is elegantly dressed, from the Izod shift dress to the Belgian loafers. She has big dark sunglasses. Adriatic. Dramatic. If I weren't so crippled with dignity, I'd say hello to her and see if she and Dad might talk to each other. I'm thinking it would be great. He'd be all set, at least for the weekend. But I don't know how to say hello to adorable strangers, never have. My whole life I've agonized, paralyzed with fear as they've passed me by. She's about to do so right now.

But then Dad sits forward and calls out to her, "Isn't it a gorgeous day?"

She stops, removes her sunglasses, looks him over, realizes he is nobody she knows, then nods. The slightest smile lifts her perfectly made-up face.

"Yes, lovely." She has a European accent and a whispery tone, kind of Zsa Zsa meets Jackie O—the soft voice of a woman used to having men lean in to hear her.

"And I see you're reading the *New York Times*?" Oh no. I know what's coming.

"Dad, please don't," I mutter. But I can't stop him. I can never stop him.

"My son writes for the *Times*."

"Oh?" she says. "That's terrific. Good for you."

She's chilly and divine. My head starts projecting a video of their courtship and romance, ending in a life together in a well-appointed Gatsby mansionette on the water.

"Is that a Slavic accent?" Dad asks.

"I'm originally from Hungary."

"I knew you sounded like a Gabor! Any chance you know them?"

*Bad question, Dad. And don't come on so hard with a European. You have to hold back.* The smile fades from her face as she puts her sunglasses back on.

"No," she says. "I don't. And I have to go." I guess she did the math and figured out that this man isn't for her. Didn't care for the sneakers, faded plaid pants. Or maybe she already has someone. Dad is not bothered by her *froideur.* I am cringing.

"And you live in the area?"

*Enough, let her go, Dad, Leave the nice European lady alone.*

"Yes, I do. It's been nice talking to you. Have a good day."

"Hope to see you again!" he calls after her.

Then she's on her way, leaving us in a subtle cloud of good perfume. I'm displeased.

"What a snob," I say.

"Oh, come on," he says. "You can't take it so seriously."

But I do. I'm livid. How dare she? This is my father we're talking about. A man who only wishes everyone well, a friendly face who likes to chat to pass the time. If I'm rude to him and dismissive at times, it's because I'm allowed to be. I'm his son.

"Why do I care so much, Dad? Why do I get so involved in your dating travails? Is it because I don't want you to end up with some fishwife from Flushing?"

He laughs. His hazel eyes sparkle in the sunshine.

I tell him I'd hate to see him get hurt.

"Look, I'm not going to get involved with anybody you don't approve of one hundred percent," he says. "I'm going to keep looking until everything is copacetic. But tell me something, Bobby. After all the talk about *my* dating, what's your news in the romance department? Anything to report?"

"Dating? Me? What are you, kidding? I've got nothing. As usual."

"Well," he says as he sits back on his bench, "maybe you're dating vicariously through me, and it gives you a thrill."

"Ha-ha, Dad! Very funny! Very funny!"

Later, after I leave him and am sitting on the train back to the city, looking at another weekend with not a kiss or a cuddle in sight, I wonder if he might be right.

Am I dating vicariously through him?

## CHAPTER 3

# Dog Date Afternoon

What to wear to a date at a dog run? Houndstooth? Wrong season. I head out in plaid Bermudas and black T-shirt to find the streets of the West Village teeming with men still in their thirties and boldly baring their hard-won physiques. I look and look away.

I should lose ten pounds. I'm not my ideal *gay* weight, okay?

But it's been over a month since the last dating disaster, so I have to try.

This one never even spoke on the phone with me. We made all the arrangements by e-mail. I know nothing more about him than that he lives downtown, works as a stagehand, and has a well-toned torso posted on his profile. He suggested we meet at the dog run at Madison Square Park so he can bring his along. Seems like a good idea to me. Why not have a friendly nonverbal third party around as a conversation starter?

I cross Thirty-third Street and enter the park, shaded with locust trees, and find the only unoccupied bench. It faces Jenny's Dog Run, a dusty fenced-in patch of dirt filled with thin youngish people and their canine companions, all clean, lively, and well behaved. I'm not a dog person. But as I watch people cuddling old beagles, throwing sticks to young Jack Russells, and stroking glossy Irish setters, I wonder if there isn't something to the love between owner and pet that I'm missing in my life. Would having a dog teach me about unconditional love, make me a better and happier person? I bet it would make it easier to get some attention on the street. Maybe I could just rent one.

Hey. I think that's my date, Greg, over there. Yes. He's entering the park in cutoffs that show nice legs. He's balding, but that's no surprise—I already saw his photos—and he's actually doing it very well: one of those shaved gay heads. I wave. He's got the coloring I love—florid skin that redheaded guys get from the sun. And great arms, not meticulously muscular, but somewhere between toned and buff. Woof.

"Greg?"

"Bob?"

"Yeah. Hi! And who's this?"

The dog is a black wiggly blur, all snout and tail.

"This is Scooter," he says.

"What kind of dog is he?"

"A Portuguese water dog."

"Adorable," I say, voice high and a little forced. "Hi, Scooter!"

I don't have to lie. The dog is adorable. He looks like the archetypal happy dog, the kind that used to fill pages of elementary-school reading books. Still, when I hold my hand out to touch Scooter, it is tentatively. Ever since I was a child and saw a cocker spaniel bite my mother's hand (she loved dogs), I have been cautious

"Yes, that's my good boy," Greg is telling Scooter, who is licking his face. Then he lets him have a nice long drink from his bottle of Evian. Do people share water bottles with dogs? He gives Scooter another drink and takes one himself. What about me? I could use a drink right now. But he doesn't offer me one.

"You two are close, huh?" I say.

"Yeah, totally," he replies, as he nuzzles Scooter. "We sleep together every night."

Now Scooter is barking at us, sharp teeth showing—an edge of violence that makes me nervous. But I keep smiling.

"He wants to play," Greg tells me. "We'll be right back."

Inside the dog run, while he throws a tennis ball over and over for his dog to retrieve, I watch with a smile plastered on my face. Alien to me as this guy's relationship is with his dog, and odd as it is to see him share his Evian, it doesn't mean I don't admire him for it. He seems like a nice person. But when we try to converse, it goes nowhere.

"Look at those nails, Scooter," he coos. "I think we're going to have to give them a clipping and polish when we get home. And what about a nice bath? Would you like a nice cool, minty bath, boy? We'll make it a full spa day for you, how about that?"

I'm smiling, but thinking, *What about me?*

A half hour passes; my heart's still pounding the way it always does around handsome men who aren't right for me. I pet the dog as he kisses him. I'm not getting anything out of this three-way. In fact, I feel invisible.

"I think it's time for lunch," he says.

"I'll walk with you," I chirp.

Stepping out from under the trees and into the intersection of Twenty-third and Broadway, we are blasted by summer sun. Greg bends down and, with biceps flexing, picks up his dog, all sixty pounds of him, and holds him in his thick, freckled arms.

"What's wrong?" I ask.

"His paws are sensitive to hot cement," he tells me.

That can't be normal. We wait to cross the street. In front of a deli, instead of putting the dog down, he turns to me and asks, "Will you hold him while I go in?"

Will I hold his dog? Is he kidding me?

"Oh sure," I say. "Take your time."

So now I'm standing on the corner of Twenty-first Street and Fifth Avenue with a big black curly-haired, hypoallergenic dog in my arms. I haven't held anyone, or even gotten this close to anyone, in a long time. There have been no babies in my life to hold. Or men. So I guess it was my mother who was the last person I held like this, mostly to help her out of cars and taxis, sometimes out of chairs as well. It's a shocking thing when you realize a parent needs help getting up and has to be lifted. But imagine how *she* felt, this woman who wanted to get around on her own but could not anymore.

"Okay, Mom, are you ready?"

"Bobby, I'm so embarrassed. It's such a terrible thing to get old."

We were in the ladies' room of a medical building in the city. I had taken her to see a new blood specialist. She went to use the bathroom and could not get off the toilet. So there I was, hoping no women would come in and find me and shriek. She struggled to push herself up against the wall, but the stall had no safety bar, and with nothing to hold on to, she kept sinking down. "Umph," she sighed. It was hopeless. I had to get in there. I had her put her arms around my neck, and in one quick motion, I leaned down into her, counted to three, and, using all my body weight, pulled her up. It was a little like dancing, with our faces so close we were cheek to cheek. She stepped forward and steadied herself. I helped her pull up her pants, holding my breath.

"There we are," I said. "All set."

"Thank you," she sighed. "I don't know what I'd do without you."

In fact, she'd been making do without much help from any of us for too long. Later, at our appointment, her new blood specialist was shocked to hear she was living in a big suburban house without a visiting nurse or any kind of aid. He was even more shocked to learn that she had a healthy husband. Why wasn't he overseeing her care?

We said good-bye to the doctor, and I called Dad on my cell phone to tell him Mom would be heading home to Long Island. "No, you should take her to an emergency room in the city," he said. We were in the doctor's waiting area now, end of a long day. Outside there was an early summer deluge. Mom was worn-out and breathing heavily.

"You don't think I should send her home? I have a car service to take her."

"I'm telling you, Bobby, do not send her back to this house tonight."

"Why? The doctor says she can go home. It's not an emergency. She's just weak. She doesn't need the hospital."

"No! No hospitals!" my mother was yelling. I don't blame her. She'd seen enough of them. And this was her last week in her home of fifty years. In another week she'd be moving—or, I should say, my brother and I would be moving her against her wishes (with Dad) to an assisted-living place located near us in Manhattan.

"Dad, she wants to come home. Let her come home."

"She doesn't belong in this house," he insisted. "She belongs in a hospital."

I felt sorry for him. And angry. And guilty. Was I sending her home because I didn't want to spend the week running to her hospital in the city? Maybe I should have been offering to spend the week on Long Island to help him help her. I'd been careful to keep a distance from the disaster their domestic life had become. Once a week was all I gave. "Sorry, Dad, but she's coming home to you now, period. End of conversation!"

I clicked off my cell phone and turned to her. "Okay, Mom, ready? Let's go."

Once again, she couldn't get up. But I let her try for the sake of her dignity.

"Lean forward, and use your legs," I coached.

The look on her face was of intense focus, as if she could will her worthless body up off the waiting room couch. But it was no good. The doctor's office was closing, the staff walking past us, unaware of our awkward situation. It was like drowning within plain sight of lifeguards on a beach. We were invisible and helpless.

But why was I impatient? Was it her fault she had gotten sick so young and lived ten years in such a debilitated state, with a blood disease that causes the body to make too many red cells and has no known treatment? Was it her fault she was pretty once and now had given up on her looks entirely, unwilling to exercise or make herself stronger? Her troubles were a downer. Like Dad, I yearned to be weightless and responsibility-free. I wondered how much longer she would suffer and, by her suffering, make us suffer.

"Okay, Mom, we really have to get out of here," I said gently.

And for the second time in an hour, I leaned down, embraced her, and—one, two, three!—lifted her up. When she was on her feet, I gave her a pat on the back.

"Good job," I said. I should have kissed her forehead. I should have held her in my arms and hugged her gently for a long time, and told her how much I loved her.

Now there is a dog in my arms. And the sky has suddenly become overcast, and a cool wind picks up on Fifth Avenue. Leaves on trees shiver. Garbage flies, men hold on to their baseball caps, women hold down their skirts. Everyone and everything is so light in a big wind. But this dog is not. He's heavy. He's panting. But not squirming. He seems to like how I'm holding him in my arms. And he's warm against me. He licks my face. Gross as it is, I laugh at the affection. "What a sweetheart you are," I whisper.

A few minutes later, I am saying good-bye to dog and owner.

The dog turns to look at me as I go. His owner does not.

CHAPTER 4

# Gracie Gravlax

The next week, on a Wednesday, I find myself waiting in front of a Broadway theater among an elderly matinee crowd. I'm meeting Dad to see a revival of the musical *Nine*. My brother treated him to a few tickets for Father's Day to use as he wished. It's a show I've wanted to see, so I'm grateful he's invited me to join him. But where is he? Why is he always late? Is he driving around and around looking for a parking spot because he refuses to pay for a lot? There he is, finally. In plaid pants and a beige V-neck that hangs too long. And who is that with him? A nice-looking woman is at his side.

"Bob! Hiya! This is Gracie," he tells me. "My favorite bridge partner."

I'm thrown but don't miss a beat. "Hello! Nice to meet you," I say, extending a hand.

Hers is cold to the touch. "My pleasure," she tells me.

"Let's go get our seats," Dad says. "We'll chat inside. Follow me."

We move into the warm sea of seniors, shuffling along slowly, shoulder to shoulder. Everyone's talking at once. It's like being in a herd of very slow-moving sheep.

"She's the most advanced child in her preschool," I hear one woman tell her friend.

"But does she speak any foreign languages?" the friend replies.

Dad looks happy. He's got his date. He's got his catch of the day, his Gracie Gravlax. Me? I'm anxious to see this musical. But I don't like the idea of being the third wheel here. Not at all.

"Here, Bob," he says. "Why don't you sit between us so I can be on the aisle?"

But I didn't come here to talk to *her*. I give her the sub-tlest once-over. She's dressed decently enough in seer-sucker skirt, white button-down blouse, white clip-on earrings, and white sandals with a sensible little heel. Dressed a little better than my mother would dress— better fabrics, better accessories, but not quite as pretty. I don't have much to ask this woman. But I know I have to try.

"So where are you from?" I ask, putting down my *Playbill*.

"Great Neck," she says, nothing more.

"Oh. And how did you and Dad meet?"

"At a bridge game at the community pool."

I might as well be the father in the living room giving her the third degree.

"Gracie is one of the top players," Dad interjects. "But,

Bob, why don't you tell us what you're working on? You have your *Times* column this week?"

*Dance, Bobby! Dance for the nice lady! Make your father proud!*

Mercifully, the lights go down, and the conversation is finished.

*Nine* is a sophisticated revival of a musical about a narcissistic womanizer having a middle-aged crisis. As I watch the dashing leading man move across the stage, as seductress after seductress descends a staircase to woo him, I find myself wishing I had that many options. Then, I realize that even my father is more like this Casanova character than I am. At least he's in the game. "I want to be young, I want to be old," the leading man sings, looking like a circus master in a ring full of lovers. "I am lusting for more, should I settle for less?" The women come and go, negligees swirling, high heels clicking, hairdos blowing. At one point, all are shouting, "Me! Me!" like desperate bridesmaids hoping to catch the bouquet.

At intermission, I rush outside for coffee to avoid any conversation.

But after the show is over, Dad will not let me go home. As we leave the theater, I feel as if I'm in a netherworld. I am not even thirty blocks from where I live downtown, and yet, where in the world am I right now? Am I really out with my father and a woman who isn't my mother? It was always disorienting enough when I took my parents around Manhattan, which I still think of as a parent-free zone. Now this? It's too much.

When was the last time I went to a Broadway show with my parents anyway? I think it was Mother's Day, five years ago, when Mom could still get around. We ditched

a dull show at intermission. I took them up to Central
Park. It was in full bloom, and I knew what I wanted to
show them—the red-tailed hawks nesting over a fancy
apartment window on Fifth Avenue. As usual, there was
a big group of birders watching from the park's reflect-
ing pond. "Would you like to look through my telescope?"
one asked my mother. She was delighted. To her, a small-
town girl with a suburban life who believed that there
was nowhere more beautiful than Long Island in the
springtime, the city was often about harsh moments and
brusque strangers. But here were these friendly nature
lovers under blossoming dogwoods eager to tell her about
their precious hawks. Even my father, usually opposed
to anything natural, could not help but be charmed. My
mother watched those hawks for a long time, cooing and
oohing as one left the nest and flew out over Central Park
in search of a pigeon or rat. "You always have something
to show us, honey, don't you?" she said, as they departed
later. It made me feel wonderful. She always made me
feel adored.

With Dad the adoration is more complicated. Why
would he want me along on this first date anyway? It's
so weird. But I guess it's only fair to give this Gracie a
chance. We cross Times Square with the matinee mob,
and then sit down in an empty Mexican restaurant Dad
chooses. It smells of disinfectant.

"Now was this the first time you'd seen *Nine*?" he asks
his Gracie Gravlax.

She says it was and that she found the script weak and
the songs unmemorable.

"I can't disagree totally," Dad says. "But overall, I
thought it was a great show."

I'm thinking it would be nice for her to say she enjoyed it, since the tickets were ninety bucks each. But she just drinks her Diet Coke and looks at her little wristwatch with grosgrain strap. There is something humorless, brittle about this Gracie, with her hairdo that looks as if one match would burn it off in a fireball. Her answers are too curt. Her countenance grim, her pale lipstick applied just so. She is graceful but ungracious. Dad starts to look sulky. Maybe I can change this vibe.

"Hey, Dad, hear any good jokes lately?"

He raises an eyebrow—indicating mischief—and replies that, in fact, he has one.

"Would you like to hear it?"

"Go ahead," Gracie says.

He clears his throat. "Three nuns die at the same time and end up at Saint Peter's gate together. 'But before I can let you in, Sisters,' Saint Peter says, 'I have to ask you each one question.' So he turns to the first nun and says, 'Your question is: Who was the first man?' She says, 'Oh, that's easy—Adam.' And Saint Peter says, 'Come on in, Sister, come on in!' Then he turns to the second nun and asks, 'Your question, Sister, is: Who was the first woman?' and the second nun says, 'Oh that's easy—Eve!' And he says, 'Come on in, Sister, come on in!' Finally, he turns to the third nun and says, 'And now can you please tell me, Sister, what were Eve's very first words to Adam?' So the third nun thinks awhile, scratches her head, and says, 'Wow, that's a hard one!' And Saint Peter says, 'Come on in, Sister, come on in!'"

It takes a moment to get it, then I laugh. I don't know where he gets these obscene jokes, but he has a bunch of them, and is always adding more to his repertoire. My mother, the prim librarian, couldn't help but light up and laugh when she heard them.

"Wow, nice one," I say as I pat his back. "Obscene *and* blasphemous."

"Happy to share," he says as he finishes his ginger ale. "I knew you'd like it."

Gracie is not laughing. She's not even smiling. Her grimace has become more pronounced. "A little rude for my taste," she says. "But isn't it time to get going?"

She buttons her cardigan and picks up her handbag. Dad pays the bill and follows her to the restaurant's exit. He holds the door for her, still trying to play the role of the gentleman suitor, even though it's clear to me he is entirely unsuitable for her.

I follow behind them onto the sidewalk, crowded at rush hour. He walks with her in front of me, still chatting her up in his amiable way, as she nods and barely responds.

I am seething. Who the hell is this woman to think she's so superior? Doesn't she get how funny my father is? Doesn't she see how handsome he is, what a catch he is? Just who the hell does she have in the wings who would be better than my Joe Morris?

"I guess she just wasn't looking to be particularly pleasant," Dad tells me on the phone later that night, when we are doing our postmortem on the afternoon.

"Well, I hope she was grateful for the ticket," I say.

"Not particularly," he says. "She found the show disappointing."

"What a pill," I say.

"A lot of these woman are hard to take," he says.

"So that's the end of Gracie?"

"We'll see."

"What do you mean? You're not taking her out *again*, are you?"

"We're in the same bridge group, and she's not a bad player. I can't afford to alienate her. A good duplicate player is harder to come by than you think."

A few days later, however, he loses her for good when he shows up late for a game. She tells him it's inconsiderate. He says he's sorry but life's too short to take things so seriously. They bicker. It escalates. Smoke comes out of her ears, fire out of his mouth. He tells her he's who he is, take it or leave it. She says she'd prefer to leave it, and turns and walks away. "She refuses to take my calls now," he says.

"Just as well, Dad. She was no bargain. Got anyone else lined up?"

"No," he says. "I'm dry right now. At a total loss."

He sounds sad. I can't have that. I won't have that. So I pull out a piece of paper with a number on it and offer up Florence, the lady with all the fancy real estate whom I had dismissed as too fancy when she was suggested as a match for him. Suddenly, he's cheerful. Another prospect! He's going to call her right away.

"I'll let you know what happens," he says. "I'm very grateful."

"You better be on your best behavior with this one," I say. "I won't have you embarrassing me. She lives on Fifth Avenue, you know."

"I know."

"So wear a clean shirt when you see her."

"Okay."

"And, Dad, don't ask for a doggy bag at dinner."

"Anything else?"

"Yes. Do not under any circumstances let her see the inside of your car."

"I'll take that under advisement."

"And don't do all the talking at dinner. Give her a chance to tell you about herself."

"I'll do my best, sir. Over and out for now."

# CHAPTER 5

## Dating Games

One day, when I'm running out of ways to entertain myself while entertaining my father, I bring him an application for *Who Wants to Marry My Dad?*, a new network reality show. I'm not naive. I know the kind of Dads they're looking for. David Hasselhoff Dads. Bruce Willis Dads. Randy, divorced Dads. Dads who are catnip to hot broads in their late thirties, women who are, like most of my single women friends, a volatile combination of picky and desperate. At a certain point, any man can look reclaimable, I guess. One of my editors tells me that, when he was in high school, his father, a free-spirited anthropology professor, started supplementing his income by working as an exotic male dancer. And the women were all over him, a constantly changing cast of chorus girls. That's the kind of father who's reality-TV-ready, not mine.

It's a warm summer afternoon, and we are sitting on the balcony of the Centra, application and pen in hand. The building is its usual ecosystem of widowed wildlife. Birds everywhere, and a few old mallards with droopy feathers. But mostly it's a female population. There are great blue-haired herons who fish through their handbags for lipstick, and adorable clucking hens who gossip and knit. Loons with jet black dye jobs. Plump robins and mynah birds with sharp Bronx accents that my father finds unpleasant. They flock to the dining hall and elevators. They perch at card tables, picking at cookies and decaffeinated tea—well-dressed women with standards, glancing over at us. Most are attractive, like so many women in Great Neck. "Nice-looking ladies," I tell Dad.

He shakes his head. "Not what I'm looking for," he mutters.

Everyone in this building, to his mind, is too senior for him, too over the hill. Actually, many are not. They just happen to live here like he does because it's easier than living alone. But he sees himself as Joe-on-the-Go, just using the place as a perch, not a nest. He doesn't want to face the fact that he's elderly. Life still interests him.

So we turn to the *Who Wants to Marry My Dad?* application, making sure to lower both his age and weight. Some of the questions require little thought. "What's the main quality you look for in a potential mate?" I ask him. "Flexibility," he answers. "Okay, I'll put that down," I say. Of course I'd like to suggest that "submissive" would be a more accurate response, but I don't editorialize. To the question, "What kind of person will you absolutely not date?" his response is "Fat."

"Do your children's opinions affect who you date?"

"Yes, absolutely."

Okay. But if he relies on my opinions, he might end up alone the rest of his life. That certainly seems to be the direction I'm heading.

"What was the craziest date you've ever been on?"

"Probably the time I ended up in my friend Jack's bed at Bard College," he says, smiling at the memory. "He wasn't in it at the time. But he showed up in the middle of the night with a girl. My presence took all the romance out of his evening."

"So I'll just put down ménage à trois, okay?"

"Sure, why not?" he laughs.

I don't know why I can't picture my father in his twenties having dating shenanigans and high-jinx when he's having all kinds of dating shenanigans sixty years later.

"When was that date? Were you playing the field at the time?"

"It was 1949, after college, just before I met your mother. I dated a lot in those days. But mostly I found that the women I got set up with were nothing extra."

"And Mom was something extra?

He sits up straight. His smile becomes almost sad, remembering her as young.

"Yes. She was gorgeous, a lovely country girl compared to the ones I was meeting. She didn't come loaded down with a lot of problems."

"So did you have to woo her?"

"The summer before we got married I was on Long Island and she was upstate with her family. We wrote letters because long-distance calls were so expensive."

He makes it sound easy. But I remember my mother telling me he was hard to nail down. He made it up to see her that summer only a couple of times. She was even in the hospital for surgery and he didn't come up. She'd write him lighthearted letters as "Your Lonesome Gal," telling him she loved him. Then she'd thank him profusely when he did finally drive up to visit. My mother had no shortage of romantic opportunities. But there was something about my father—this funny, earnest bachelor—that rang her chimes. They met at a Zionist Club meeting at the Bay Shore Jewish Center. It didn't hurt that he was a good-looking man with his own law practice. More than that, he had a sense of fun and romance, and an ability to turn anything into a sing-along. He was sentimental and affectionate, something almost impossible to find in men back then.

"I appreciate your coming up, honey, thanks so much," my mother wrote him from her parents' house in 1950. "You know if marriage is a matter of give and take, I think we both have what it takes." Somehow, they did, but without her ability to be flexible and easily amused, their marriage would have never have lasted so long.

There are more questions on the *Who Wants to Marry My Dad?* application, some too cringe-inducing for me to ask aloud. ("Describe a romantic evening" and "What is the biggest contribution to your sexual views?" Who the hell would ever ask such a thing of his father?) It's easier to ask him to list three talents he has. Dad thinks a moment, then says, "Put down making up parodies, dancing, and bridge."

"Okay. Last question, Dad. They want you to list your bad habits."

"And how much room do they leave?"

"Two lines," I laugh.

"Write small," he says.

So I do. And while he lists a few, a longer list accumulates in my mind. He's always late. He's sloppy and absentminded. He chews with his mouth open and is prone to unforeseeable rages over nothing. He is controlling, willful, profligate in advice giving and matchmaking, even when people aren't asking and don't want to be set up. He'd rather talk than listen. He loves changing plans. He keeps you on the phone, even when it's obvious you don't want to talk. He writes postcards to people he hasn't seen in ages. His bridge habit is actually an addiction that makes him miserable when he can't play. And when he does, he gives too much advice to his partners. He remains a rabid Republican. He veers into the middle lane when driving. And lately, I've been appalled to see that, in addition to the ballpoint pens he keeps in the front pocket of his shirt, he has toothpicks that he pulls out at all the wrong moments. Like now. We are sitting among his fellow Centra residents, all out enjoying the late-afternoon sun on his building's big terrace, and he starts picking at his teeth and making a sucking noise. Appalling.

"Dad, would you mind? Save it for your bathroom."

Fortunately, he doesn't take it personally today. But pity the poor date who dares to criticize him if he's in the wrong mood. Who wants to marry my dad? There are days when I think nobody. And the more I talk about his dating travails to my friends, the more I hear similar stories. It turns out I'm not the only bemused child sucked into a senior father's mating melee. One friend has an upstanding dad who picked up a woman on a commuter train and dropped her straight into the family without so much as a word of explanation. Two sisters I know are totally flummoxed by a shy Connecticut father in his seventies, very recently widowed, who has taken up with a married woman in her forties. I hear stories of men whose dying wives leave them lists of women they approve of for dating after they're gone. I hear about an "intervention," in which a family removes a father from a woman about to marry him and take him for all his money. One friend tells me that when her rapscallion dad moved into her apartment after his fifth divorce, he started lobbying her prettiest friends to set him up with their mothers. "I ended up racing to the phone every time it rang so he wouldn't answer it," she says. "It was horrible."

My favorite story is one about a friend's father in his late seventies, recently widowed, and also legally blind for thirty years. At his country club, the women circle around him like ducks to bread. One widow, in her seventies, white-haired and overweight, flirts with him, and he flirts back. She recently confided to my friend that she loves flirting with her father because the last time he was able to see her she was still young and thin.

In June, for my Father's Day column, I write about Dad's big hunt for new love in his old age, touching on both the amusement of knowing he still has so much potential ahead of him and the unseemliness of the notion that, at eighty, he wants to have what he calls intimacy with women. He's a good sport about it and doesn't seem to mind being material for me. He's always trying to tell me what to write about anyway. So there's some satisfaction for him in being my topic. And the column gets a good response. One reader, a woman with a seventy-one-year-old mother, is moved to write:

Dear Bob,

I have to admit, it was a bit of a shock when my mother called one day with the news that she'd started seeing someone. It was bracing, and at times even comical to hear her dating postmortems—how his sweet nothings made her hearing aid squeal, how he was lusting (lusting, Mom?) for her body (they definitely had it going on in the chemistry department). But ultimately, I took heart in their growing romance.

Such whirlwind love affairs are too often relegated to the young. What I've learned is that falling in love and desiring companionship isn't the sole domain of the young at all, but something we crave regardless of age. The year Mom married, she had two friends, both in their eighties, who were smitten. One tied the knot that summer, another, at age eighty-five, went through a protracted divorce to leave her empty sixty-year marriage so she could be, at last, with a man who truly made her happy: her ninety-two-year-old beau. In hindsight, Mom's romance has left me feeling hopeful. I realize that growing older doesn't preclude our ability to tap into that heady, butterflies-in-the-stomach feeling of love. With the recent collapse of my own marriage, I take heart in the notion that I, too, have "all this potential" ahead of me.

Personally, I think you're too focused on what you might lose instead of seeing what you and your dad stand to gain. So buck up and quit thinking your father needs you to manage his life. My guess is that he'll do just fine out there and likely fall madly in love with someone who won't be your mother—but who will ultimately make him happy.

And isn't that what we want for those we love?

Yes of course it's about his happiness, not mine. But that doesn't mean it's easy to stop passing judgment. I have more opinions than anyone I know.

So many, it seems there's hardly any room for feelings.

CHAPTER 6

# Regular Joe and
# Fifth Avenue Florence

My father's black tassel loafers are not the kind you see in a doorman building on Fifth Avenue. They have a kind of discount store quality to them. I have to rely on my imagination here if I'm to get a picture of his big date with Florence. The only thing I know is that, much to my surprise, the woman who set them up has reported back to me he was found to be "a delightful conversationalist." So now I'm all ears for his report. What does this Florence look like? What does her apartment look like? What details do I get from him? Nothing! For all the times he wants to tell me about all the things in his life that don't interest me at all, now, *now*, when I'm dying to know every single detail, he is being terse and vague.

"I just picked her up at her apartment and took her to a nice dinner," he's telling me.

"So where'd you go?"

"An Italian place she likes."

"Which one? Gino's? Serafina?"

"I can't remember. Food was overpriced. Place was overcrowded, like everywhere else in the city. Our next date will be in Great Neck."

"Did you pay?"

"We went Dutch."

"Oh no, Dad! Why?"

"She insisted."

"So was she nice?"

"She was fine. Younger than me. Good figure. Very bright."

"So what did you talk about?"

"I can't remember. But listen, the ball game's starting. We'll catch up tomorrow."

How dare he? I'm the one who gives him the bum's rush to get him off the phone, not vice versa. And what is wrong with me anyway, obsessing about his date with the fancy rich lady? Now I can't sleep. In my restless mind I'm reviewing his night with Florence. My version has the scratchy and jumpy quality of an old home movie.

Here's how I imagine it:

He pulls his junk mobile up to an imposing residential building on Fifth Avenue, where he finds a convenient parking space. Miracle on Eighty-fourth Street! Suddenly, his tenuous relationship with Manhattan—the crowds, the dirt, the Democrats, the cost of parking—is all resolved for the evening, and he feels happy and light on his feet. He's in a new white button-down shirt, clean chinos, and a blue blazer just back from the dry cleaner. Jaunty. Dating is starting to teach him to dress better. If it weren't for his gimpy walk, he might be Gene Kelly. The stern doorman shows him right in. He whizzes up in a wood-paneled elevator, pulling a dirty comb from the pocket of his blazer to get his hair into place. There, at the top floor, is a woman looking fifteen years his junior, hair auburn and recently done, waiting at her door.

"Joe? Hello. You're late. I'm Florence. Come in!"

She's brusque. He could be daunted. She looks, as he likes to say, hoity-toity in a white linen suit and—what are those, pearls?—like some of the snootier Palm Beach dames who don't give him the time of day. But he's in his easy-breezy mode tonight, looking good, feeling good, allergies well medicated with a cocktail of pills. And she hasn't had a date in months, so why not give this gentleman a fair shake?

"Please pardon the mess," she tells him. "I'm packing for Sun Valley."

"Don't think anything of it," he says.

He wonders to himself, *What is she talking about?* There's no mess. The place is immaculate. The kind of home he's seen only on TV. Views of the park. Grand piano with Liberace candelabra. Big vases of flowers like he's seen only at Ritz-Carlton brunches. A lady named Inez in an apron brings him a whiskey sour and tiny bowl of warm nuts. He uses the only Spanish he knows to tell her, *"Muchas gracias."* The tumbler is made of heavy crystal. And those oil paintings with bronze lights over them are by someone famous, he thinks. One is of a bespectacled, imposing bald man.

"That was my late husband, Art," she says.

"Good-looking guy," Dad says. "What was his line of work?"

Okay. Five minutes in, and he's already broken two cardinal rules of first dates: Don't inquire about the ex, and never lead by talking about what anyone does for a living.

But she doesn't seem to mind. She sips her dry martini, big gold bracelets jangling, and explains he was a manufacturer—gynecological instruments—something that leaves even Joe Morris without much to say. So there's a moment of silence.

But then the conversation moves on from Sun Valley, a place where she spends summers and Dad has never been, to Palm Beach, where they both go for the winter.

"Whereabouts are you located there?" he asks.

"Sunset Avenue, near The Breakers."

"Terrific area. I eat at Chuck and Harold's all the time."

"I used to more often. But the new chef tends to overcook things."

"Works for me. I like everything well done."

"Well, it's a free country," she says.

The woman, this Florence, is no slouch. She runs with discriminating crowds in the three places she has her homes. And she doesn't miss a trick when it comes to assessing new people. For instance, she notices, as she and my father walk to Madison Avenue for dinner, that this gentleman caller, Joe Morris, is not as quick moving as she would have liked. And yet there's something boyish about him. His skin is almost without a wrinkle, and there's something about him that's smooth without being slick, open and affable, and she likes the way he talks as if he hasn't a care in the world, a kind of Jewish Tony Bennett. Okay, she could live without the slights about Muslims and the Pope he makes over dinner. And she finds it a little surprising when he pulls some sweetener from his wallet and dumps it in his glass of wine. And perhaps it would be more pleasant if his table manners were better, and he finished chewing before speaking. Also, those eyeglasses—just like the ones George Bush Sr. wears—why are they so smudged? But as they chat about bridge, Palm Beach, Great Neck, and, of course, me, she can't help but be a little more than charmed. She finds my dad delightful, even when he pockets some Equal packets from the table.

It isn't until Dad is walking her home, sweetly crooning all the lyrics to "I Love New York in June," that she gets a little twisting in her gut. That can't be something romantic stirring down below her silk blouse, can it? In front of her building, with her doorman watching protectively, he wishes her a lovely summer in Sun Valley, kisses her hand, and finishes by crooning "I'll Be Seeing You." She walks into her elevator, flushed, with hearts, stars, and little twittering birdies circling around her dignified head.

At least that's how I imagine it.

So why, after she liked him, is he now talking about scaring up other dates? They only met two weeks ago. We've just gotten back to his apartment after a pleasant dinner next door at a Greek place. It's a lovely summer night, but of course every window is shut. I open them all. He frowns at the fresh air and sits down at his table, piled high with papers and pill bottles.

"So Florence wants to see you again, Dad? That's great."

"Yes, well, it's mutual. Trouble is, she's in Sun Valley all summer."

"So maybe you should fly out there for a weekend and surprise her."

"Are you kidding? That mountain altitude would be the worst thing for my heart."

"So you won't chase her, huh?"

He leans in and stares me down with a smarmy smile. "No. But I hope she's chaste because she won't be *chased* by me."

I laugh. "But why not chase her, Dad? What could be the harm?"

"Look, I'm not going to see her again until Palm Beach. That's six months away. So I'm not taking myself off the market yet, that's all."

My blood starts racing. Why does he have to ruin the first good thing to come along in his little dating derby? "Oh, for God's sake," I say. "Haven't you had enough?"

"I want someone to spend time with—someone to take to concerts."

"Well, I'm not procuring any more women for you. My pimping days are over."

He sighs and looks a little hurt. "Sorry to hear you say that. You've been so eager."

Just then I notice, beneath brochures, bills, and clippings of bridge columns, an envelope addressed to him in a very elegant script. The return address is Sun Valley. Inside, there's a vellum note card with engraved name. "Dear Joe," it reads. "Thanks so much for your delightful letter and funny lyrics. I will cherish them all summer."

"Dad? Lyrics? You wrote her a song? I want to see it."

"I made a copy, but I don't remember where I put it. What's that under the couch?"

I get up and pick up a paper, and yes—it's a typewritten ditty that says "For Florence" at the top.

"Wow! So you wrote this just for her?"

"One of several I sent."

"Really? So you two have been corresponding? Why didn't you tell me? Fantastic!"

"She seems to appreciate my humor," Dad says.

"That's great. Will you sing this one for me?"

"Sure. Why not? Give it here."

He takes the paper, holds it in his hand, clears his throat, and sings to the bouncy tune of "Darktown Strutters' Ball."

*I'll be down there waiting in a golf cart, Florence*
*Better be ready December third*
*Don't have to say a word*
*It's time for bridge and then an early dinner.*
*I feel good on my new medication*
*Gastroenterologistically*
*It'll be like we're on a cruise*
*Eating not drinking 'cause we're Jews*
*December third when I find you in Palm Beach!*

I applaud like the parent of a child who has just spoken at a school assembly.

"Bravo! Genius, Dad! And she keeps writing back that she thinks you're funny?"

"We've kept up a good correspondence. But you know me, I love writing letters."

"Boy, this thing could really work out. It could be so great. So why don't you give yourself a break now and just knock off the dating for a while? Just focus on her!"

He shakes his head. His determined grimace annoys me.

"Look," he says. "Maybe it will work out with her, and maybe it won't. I'm not putting too many eggs in one basket yet. If you look under those letters from Florence, you'll find some others." I see what he means. There are all kinds of letters from everywhere on this table. I grab the whole stack, and, to my dismay, beneath the Florence letters are various letters on various stationeries in various handwritings. Appalling. It's like finding a stack of porn magazines under a son's bed.

"Who's this from, Dad?"

"Anna, from a bridge class I taught in Florida," he says. "She's in Jersey for the summer. She wants to get together in the city for lunch and a matinee."

"When?"

"I'm stalling. She's not my cup of tea."

"And who sent you this Valentine in the middle of summer?"

"Rhonda. But that's finished. Too pushy."

I should not be going on with this, but I do and find a Xerox at the bottom of the pile. He's laughing, thinks it's funny.

"And what's this, Dad? More lyrics? Are these to Florence?"

"No, they're not."

I look closer on the page and see, to my horror, that they're for Edie. Three-timing Edie!

"Why are you still writing her, Dad?"

"Why not? Those are clever, to the tune of 'Hooray for Hollywood.' Want to hear?"

"Let's have it."

*This is my weekly call*
*I hope you're hitting well on every ball*
*You're driving straight on every fairway, on every fair day*
*And that you're putting's in line!*

"Dad, I thought you said she had two other boyfriends in Philly."

"She does, but that doesn't mean I can't correspond in a platonic way."

"I can't believe you're serious."

"I'm serious about wanting to have a good time, that's all."

"But Dad, you had a great first date with Florence, and you're writing each other long letters. She gets you. So do yourself a favor and focus on her, okay?"

He shakes his head.

"This is just like you to want to complicate things that could be so simple," I say.

"Look, Bobby, I like to think that I can date a thousand women until the right one comes along. I want to hear everyone's story. I think everyone I meet deserves a chance. Right now I'm going to play the field."

Fishing at the widow pond is more like it, I'm thinking. Or maybe it's drinking at the widow trough. But enough already. There's a train in ten minutes. I get up.

"Look, do what you want," I tell him. "I've got to go."

I turn in frustration and walk out his door. Of course

it's none of my business, I tell myself as I run to the railroad station. But how could he possibly disrespect what he's started, what *we* started with Fifth Avenue Florence? It's so confounding to be part of his hell-bent hunt for new love. Why can't he play by some basic rules instead of making his typical mess, which is becoming more complicated than an ice-blended mocha? How often does a classy dame come along and appreciate the barely socialized charms of Joe Morris? Then, on the train back to the city, it suddenly occurs to me that of course he'd want to play the field. I mean he *is* so open, so accepting of everyone he meets, the most accepting man I've ever known, such a *democratic* Republican.

When I was nineteen and going off to wash dishes on Fire Island one summer, he's the one who came up to my room and came out of the closet *for me*—and told me it was fine with him, as long as I was careful. I was packing a duffel bag while listening to the Grateful Dead, eager to escape our suburban town for another world. He sat on my bed in his tennis whites. "I wanted to talk to you about something," he said.

"What's up, Dad?"

"This is a little hard to say. It's just that your mother and I have noticed you didn't have a girlfriend in school this year."

I put down what I was packing. The record ended. The room went silent.

"Yeah," I say. "No big deal."

"But I want you to know that if you like men, it's okay. All I'd ask of you is to be careful, and keep all options open in life. You mother and I love you no matter what."

I stood there, hair recently cropped short, Fire Island–style, then I resumed folding a black T-shirt with my heart pounding. Did he really just say that? Where was it coming from? I'd had a girlfriend my whole senior year of high school, so why would he suspect anything just a year later? It was the 1970s, years before the country would grow comfortable with the word *gay*. And yet, he was fine about it. He knew, and with this one conversation, this man I thought was so imperceptive made my life much easier.

I now had nothing to hide, and a burden that could have gone on for years was gone.

"I imagine it must not be easy, Bobby," he said. "But I know you'll figure it out."

"Thanks, Dad," I whispered. "I appreciate it."

Then he patted my shoulder and left my room, and my life as an adult began.

Years later, when I was a struggling freelancer and had to move back home because I couldn't afford rent in the city, instead of discouraging me, he told me he admired me for doing what I wanted to do with my life. There was nothing I did that didn't make him proud. He recorded every one of my junior-high band concerts and played them back as if they were the Boston Pops. In my late thirties, I found myself during lonely summers back on Long Island playing trombone in a little community band in Sag Harbor. My parents would drive over on Tuesday nights to hear me play. I grumbled to them my whole childhood about my music lessons, but as a middle-aged man in that silly little band, in a silly little uniform, I was giving something back to them after all the lessons they'd paid for—their beloved, old-time popular music.

We weren't a great band. In fact, at times we were close to awful. But my parents looked so proud as they listened. There were so many little things I did that made them happy. They always made it so easy.

So how, I wondered as my train pulled into Penn Station, did I grow up to be such a judgmental snob?

# CHAPTER 7

# Love's Loser's Lost

Summer rolls along. Dad's right hip, which he is planning to have replaced if he can get clearance from his heart specialist, bothers him, but that doesn't keep him from getting around, zipping from one diversion to the other like an antic blue jay in a neighborhood full of birdfeeders. He's too amusement-oriented to sit still, yet he isn't as happy as he sounded over the winter in Palm Beach. He plays bridge at Great Neck's pool and at the senior center. He comes up with new duplicate partners for old chums, and writes countless letters to friends and relatives (all carbon copied for his files) about his new life alone in assisted living and his desire to get back to Florida. Not that he's suffering on Long Island. Great Neck, it seems to me, is a place where seniors are such an important demographic that they can be almost militant. They rule the library, the community center, and the aisles of Waldbaum's. You see them everywhere, waiting for buses and trains into the city. Loitering at magazine racks and at Starbucks, where they grill the staff about the confusing terminology of contemporary coffee. They are all over the *Great Neck Record*, posing with authors at local readings, and they are on the sidewalks, using their walkers as something like snowplows to clear the way. And why not? When I get to my cane-waving years, I'm going to take full advantage of the entitlement that comes with frailty. And I'm not going to have any problem with not working either. But Dad's still lonely. So I visit as much as I can stand it. We take scenic drives to Port Washington and Sands Point.

I keep trying to come up with activities that we both enjoy.

Sometimes, when I'm busy, I coax him into the city. One evening, he tries out the train, and I meet him at Penn Station to take him to dinner. I want him to enjoy himself, and to see how manageable the city is without a car. It starts out on a happy note, as I shepherd him onto the E train without a problem. Our subway car isn't crowded, and it's clean and well air-conditioned. And, thankfully, there aren't any panhandlers coming through to give him cause for one of his anti-city tirades. But then, when we get out at Fifty-third Street—holy hell—the escalator isn't working. This has never happened to me before. My heart seizes. I have no idea where an elevator is. How am I going to get my father out of this subway station? I stand in a crowd, as subways come and go past us, their overwhelming roar only adding to the anxiety. I am as lost as I've ever been. Are we going to have to walk up the longest nonmoving staircase in the city?

"I'm sorry, I don't know what else to do, Dad. Can you make it?"

"Bobby, let me ask you—what choice do I have?"

So the long climb begins. On a mercilessly unmoving escalator full of people rushing past us, he places a slightly arthritic hand on the rubber banister, lowers his head, and puts one beige vinyl loafer in front of the other. From behind him I notice a few crumbs stuck to the back of his khaki trousers. After ten steps, he's doing okay. After twenty, he's slowing way down. In fact, he has started sagging. The remaining strands of his fine white hair hang in his disgusted eyes. Pedestrians are passing on the left, checking to see if he's okay. Besides his hip problem, his heart is a worry. He's on many medications.

"I really don't think I can make it, Bobby," he moans. "It's too much for me. I don't know why I let you talk me into coming into the city. Never again."

I force myself to be solicitous, even as my temper flares.

"Rest right here for a while," I say. "We don't have to go farther until you're ready."

Ten more steps and he's grunting in a basso profundo. And in a gesture suitable for the most tragic of scenes at the Metropolitan Opera, he has slumped himself over on the railing to catch his breath. People are stopping and staring as they tromp past, looking at me in an accusatory manner. *How dare you make such an infirm old man take these stairs? What kind of son are you? Why isn't he in a cab or ambulance? Shame!*

I'm concerned for him. But also aware I have to *show* concern for him.

"Are you okay, Dad? Do you want me to get an ambulance?"

"No, no," he moans. "Just let me try to get through this nightmare."

Even now I find myself judging him for being ridiculous, then hating myself for thinking this way. I'm actually worried. Isn't it just so typical that the one night Dad has taken up my suggestion to use mass transit, this goddamn escalator stops running? What are the chances of that? It's like what my grandfather used to say in Yiddish: *Mann tracht, Gott lacht. Man plans and God laughs.* I wonder if there's a special god who oversees boomer children and elder parents? Perhaps there's a patron saint of parentalism—Saint Irwin or Sidney—who determines the weather between fathers and sons like us, one day fair and mild, the other tempestuous and hostile.

We are only halfway up this dead subway escalator on this hot summer night. There are dozens of steps still ahead of us. It is a stairway as much to heaven as hell, and a clear picture, I realize, of what's to come with my old man. When I look up at the distressingly long climb, I can't help imagining my father is ascending up into the beyond. "Just give me a minute to rest," he is gasping.

"Take all the time you want, no hurry," I reply.

People walk past us, offering helping hands, offering to call the police for us. Nobody is annoyed at us for slowing them down. This is another instance when New Yorkers show their humanity, not their bile. I used to see this with my mother all the time in her last years. One day I was taking her to a doctor near Fifth Avenue. The cab had pulled over, and she struggled to get herself on her feet. Halfway up, she'd sink backward into the cab again. The driver waited patiently, even though we were holding up traffic. "Okay, I surrender," she finally said. "Help me up."

I leaned down—one, two, three—and lifted her up. She whimpered. I grunted. Then I gave her my arm to hold as she worked to step onto the sidewalk. A curb had never looked so daunting. She was prone to falling, and any fall could be lethal. She waited, panting, as I paid the driver, who looked to be from Africa, maybe Haiti.

As he took the money, he said to me, "The grace of God."

"Excuse me?" I said.

He nodded toward my mother. "You will receive the grace of God for being a good son to your mother," he said.

"Oh," I said. "Thank you."

He was gone before I could give him an extra tip.

That was the moment I first realized that taking care of a parent in need is as much an opportunity as a responsibility, a chance to give back to the people who gave you so much. But that was then. This is now, several years later, and I'm thinking, Maybe not. What kind of son would shame his elderly father into coming into the city in the heat of summer and make him take the subway? What kind of son would make him walk up all these steps? He hates exerting himself. And just like those days when my mother was so incapable of getting anywhere, I feel so isolated and alone with him here, now, in the middle of a world that's moving so fast.

Eventually he makes it to the top, where he pants and

teeters to a bench and sits down with a gale-force sigh. I run to get him a bottle of Snapple.

"Peach," he has the energy to call after me. "Or rasp-berry! Diet!"

We have survived the ordeal.

Later, he tells me, "I hate the city because it gets you in its grip and decides things for you. On Long Island in the car, I'm the one in control of my life."

"Is that why you made such a scene at the subway station, Dad?"

"It's important to know your enemies, and New York is mine," he says. "When you hate something so much, you have to say so. It's too hard to hold back."

Unsettling as it is to consider, I'm pretty much the same way.

After dinner that night, Dad declares an end to all forays into Manhattan. And that's fine. I can visit him where he lives. I drive back and forth past Great Neck to the Hamptons, and also right past the cemetery on the Southern State Parkway where Mom is buried. Sometimes I stop in. Other times I wave as I speed past. "Hi, Mom!" I call.

This July Fourth weekend, I've been invited to stay at a friend's house in Bridgehampton. Another friend, a high-rolling Englishman, is giving a party in his cottage on an East Hampton dune. It's full of beautiful people. I talk to a famous actress and a famous actor, tell them about how I'm taking acting classes because I'm in a little show I've written. I shmooze an editor in chief. The party is full of desirable men my age. But I end up sitting alone in the dunes to watch the fireworks. "I don't care for all those colors," I hear one self-appointed critic snipe. "Yeah, it's a little much," another sighs. "The champagne hues are more subtle." Do I sound that tasteful and fussy? I hope not. In a head-spinning rush, I hit one party after the next—running sickness, I call it. And at the end of the weekend, I zip past Mom's cemetery, waving in her direction without slowing down. Then I pass right by Dad's Great Neck exit, feeling guilty, but wanting to get home. I have mail to open, calls to return, a column to start.

I'm not there long when my phone rings. I pick it up to hear a purring voice.

"Is this Bob Morris?"

"Speaking."

"Hello, Bob. My name is Kitty Levin. I got your number from Joyce Lutz at the *Times*. She said to go ahead and call. I hope you don't mind."

I don't actually know Joyce Lutz at the *Times*, but I know who she is. I'm just a freelance columnist after all, and she's a high-up executive married to a former top editor. If you get a call from a stranger dropping her name, you have to be polite.

"I'm a journalist, too," Kitty Levin is telling me. "With the *East Side Gazette*. I cover society parties. I go to them all. I'm very persuasive at getting invitations. I have photos of myself with everyone from Dr. Ruth to Lena Horne."

"That's great. Sounds like a fun gig," I say.

Why is she calling me? I hope it's not what I think it is.

"Anyone who knows me, Bob, will tell you that I'm an extremely capable woman. Now I'll tell you the purpose of this call, and I hope you don't find this presumptuous, but I read that column you wrote on Father's Day about your dad's dating life, and I wanted to know if he's still on the market. If he is, I would like his number."

"Oh. So you're calling me to get to my dad?"

"That's right. I think we could be a match. I have a good sense of these things."

"Just so I know, why do you think you'd be a match?"

"Well, I'm attractive, first of all, and amiable, and I really know how to *please* a man. I know how to make children love me, too. The only problem is I'm not young."

I'm listening to this woman. She doesn't have a tacky accent. She sounds like she might even be attractive. She lives in the right zip code, and, although she's no prize-winning journalist, she sounds pretty clever. The problem is she sounds way too aggressive. The last thing I want is an overwhelming, high-strung personality with my father just as I'm starting to find him (shocking as it is) kind of amusing to be around.

"You know, it's nice you called," I tell her. "But I think he's found someone."

"What do you mean by 'think'?"

"I mean, he's not actively dating anymore."

"Are you sure? How do you know that?"

Oh, my God. Such desperation. What part of the word *no* does she not understand?

Then I take a moment to think about it. Maybe I'm being unsympathetic. I mean, the demographics are so cruelly stacked against her. The last Census reports 20.6 million women sixty-five and older and 14.4 million men. That's ten women for every seven men, odds more terrible than what my single female friends are facing in Manhattan. But whenever I hear the phrase "casserole widows"—referring to the kind of senior woman who

shows up at a man's doorstep right after a wife has died—
I have to laugh. I shouldn't. One day I'm going to be an
old man, too. Do I want people to call me a whiny old
fruit or mutter behind my back if I'm moving too slowly
at the airport? A study cited in the paper not long ago
shows that one of the causes of frailty in the elderly is all
the joking at their expense. It's not just the fault of the
younger generation, who call lapses of memory "having
a senior moment." The elderly do it to each other. In a
culture of political correctness, senior citizens are still a
demographic wide open to every sort of ridicule.

The thing about this Kitty Levin on the phone is that
she doesn't sound elderly at all. She sounds like a dynamo.
Maybe that's the problem.

"So what do you say, Bob? Do you think your father
could handle me?"

"Look," I tell her. "Thanks for calling. Let me take your
information."

So she gives me her number, and I tell Dad about her,
warning him she's pushy and doesn't sound right for him.
But he goes and calls her anyway, and they have a nice
chat. Then he calls me with a favor to ask. I'm right in the
middle of a deadline.

"You want me to do *what*, Dad?"

"I want you to go meet her."

"Why should I do that?"

"Because she tells me that she's drop-dead gorgeous,
and I'd like to believe her, but as a lawyer I'm trained to
be skeptical."

"So now you want me to go on your dates *for* you?"

"Look, Bobby, she lives in the city, and I don't want to

drag her out to Great Neck if she's not up to snuff. I can't tell you how tired I am of taking duds to dinner."

"So then forget about her, Dad, she's not worth it."

"I suggested you could meet her Thursday morning at ten o'clock in front of that Gristedes at Eighty-sixth and Broadway. Will that work for you?"

"In your dreams, buster."

"What about a coffee shop then?"

"Are you kidding me? If you want to meet her so badly, you go. Squeeze your own melons! Kick your own tires! Besides, I still think you should hold off until you get to see if you can make a go of it with Florence. You two are still writing letters, right?"

"Yes. But, Bobby, please. Do your old man a favor. I'm lonely. I want a date this weekend. You can think about it tonight, and let me know your decision tomorrow."

I don't want to think about it. I don't want to think about him either. I want to think about my own aspirations and frustrations. I want to finish my column and talk to friends whose stunning accomplishments will make me anxious about my lack of them. I want to live in a parent-free zone this week. Still, I can't get this Kitty Levin out of my head. I keep imagining what would happen if I actually did meet her Thursday morning:

*I walk into a coffee shop. Muzak is playing "I'll Never Fall in Love Again." The place is filled with senior women, all drinking tea with lemon, and eating their toast "dry" and alone. Is that her with that teased-out hair, pink as cotton candy? She's waving. I step closer. She's very put together. Lots of makeup. But definitely not drop-dead gorgeous.* "Hi, Bob," *she's calling.* "It's me, Kitty, over here!"

*Oh, my God. Look at those pink nails, long as biscotti.*

"Come sit," *she says.* "I was scared you weren't coming. I'm on my fourth coffee. So I'm talking a little faster than usual. Would you like a cup?"

"Sounds good," *I say, and sit down at a table much too small for us.*

"Look how handsome you are," *she coos.* "I hope you get your looks from your father!" *Her perfume is a little aggressive. Her nose as flamingo-like as her hair color. She's got Jane Fonda's memoir in front of her.*

"She's a remarkable woman," *she says.*

"That's funny because my father hates everything she stands for," *I say.* "He likes his women simple, the kind who don't think or push, you know, like Laura Bush."

"Well," *she says, as she checks her pink lips in her butter knife,* "maybe he can afford to be picky. But not me. And with three women like me for every single man, I've developed a thick skin. But let me tell you something, Mr. Bob Morris, I don't care how it makes me sound. I'm not ashamed to tell you that I don't think there's anything more important in life than to love and be loved! In the end, it's all that matters, isn't it?"

"Oh, come on," *I say.* "I'm sure your life is plenty full without a man. You seem like a very self-sufficient woman."

"Oh, I am. Still, you can't imagine what it's like, wondering if you'll ever get the chance to cuddle or hold hands with anybody again. And you can't imagine what

*it's like facing so many Saturday nights alone without
even a date to look forward to."*

I don't tell her that, in fact, I can. She leans in close.
"Listen, I know what's going on here," she says. "You're
screening me for your father, aren't you? Well, that's
fine. He wants to conserve his energy, and doesn't want
to schlep into town to meet me. You're a good son to help
him out. But please, whatever you think of me, do me a
favor and let him decide for himself. Promise me you'll
tell him to give me a try. What's the harm?"

I feel horrible. Even if she's a little pushy, she's just
being honest, and besides, she is perfectly nice. Despite
my picky taste, Dad would find her attractive, and
she deserves a chance to make him happy just as he
deserves a chance to drive her crazy. But maybe I'm too
shallow, I don't know. She just isn't good enough. For
me. But I don't want to hurt her feelings. So I just smile
and nod. Then I lie.

"To be honest," I tell her, "you seem like such a youthful woman, and even though Dad is getting very agile
in his wheelchair, I worry that he'd slow you down."

There's a beat of silence, just enough for her to sit up
straighter.

"Oh, I see," she says, as she finishes her coffee, leaving a pink lipstick smear on the cup. "Well, okay then.
You know, I suspected he might be a little old for me."

Then she leans over the table real close, exposing far
too much décolletage. Her voice drops at least half an
octave, turning into something just south of sultry.

"So tell me more about your dating life, Bobby."

"Me? I don't have one. I hate dating."

*"But what does a nice mature Jewish single like you like to do on a hot July night?"*

*Oh my God. Is she . . . hitting on me now? Do I really look that old? After a lifetime of keeping love away, has it all come to this now on a Saturday night in New York?*

My computer beeps. An e-mail rouses me from my daydream.

But I can't shake the image of this woman's desperation from my head.

And then I have to wonder if I'm almost as desperate myself.

I never do go meet her. But my father keeps her in a file getting thicker by the day.

## CHAPTER 8

# Road Trip

In August, I have to be in Dartmouth for a staged reading of a doomed musical I'm writing. It's a long drive that I don't want to take on my own. I'd like to spend a couple days out of the city before getting to work up there, but staying in an inn alone isn't so appealing. For years I've been able to convince myself that traveling solo is good for the spirit and means you don't have to compromise. Now I'm tiring of it. Sure, you can bring a book to read at dinner. But you also have to be prepared to hear the sound of people getting it on in the next room. Maybe Dad and I could drive up together, I think.

What could go wrong? It takes all of a moment to project the possibilities.

He could dislike the place I book because it's old. He could throw his back out as he did on Nantucket one year,

ending up in the local clinic. A toothache is another possibility. That took down a family vacation to the Caribbean one winter. Or it could just rain, leaving us in a
room together all weekend with nothing but TV to fill
the time.

My track record for traveling with my dad isn't exactly
perfect. One summer after college, when I was a charming
combination of arrogant and broke, he and Mom picked
me up in front of a pizzeria in New Hampshire. I had just
hitchhiked down from a summer with an earthy Marxist
theater company in Vermont. We rode in his battleship-
size Lincoln Continental. I was righteous and anticorpo-
rate. The first George Bush was in office at the time. And
the word was there'd be a war for oil. So as the family
gas-guzzler crossed New England, and he checked us into
Ramada Inns and Marriotts along the way, we fought about
the Middle East and the administration's AIDS policies.
After three days we were two hissing cockroaches.

I was supposed to be reading the map while he drove.

"I told you to turn there, Dad!"

"I know you did. I heard you."

"I've got the map. You don't trust me?"

"Look, don't make a federal case out of this. My hunch
is you're wrong."

"Well, my hunch, Dad, is you're an idiot."

Even as I said it, I was sorry. He grabbed the map from
out of my hands, swerved the car into the right lane, and
ended up freaking out an elderly couple passing in a convertible. Their horn blared in anger. I felt like grabbing
him by the throat. Why? Because his politics were main-
stream? Because he preferred Marriotts to old country
inns? I'd been exposed to so much in my first years in

college—Eurotrash, Roxy Music, sushi, limousine Le-
ninism, and drugs that only the privileged could afford.
People liked me. They liked my Bermuda shorts and old-
school eyeglasses. They liked my humor and creative
outbursts—writing poems on the sides of supermarket
walls in the middle of the night, making experimental
videos and performance art that only children who were
raised to feel special could make. Many of my friends
had their parents come to campus for visits. I didn't en-
courage mine as much as I should have. I was a little embarrassed. And now, at the end of a summer of political
art-making, I had to tolerate the limited consciousness
of this Republican who sired me. He was as angry as I've
ever seen him. My mother was cowering in the back, listening to every word.

"I'm sick of your attitude. Why don't you go to hell?"

"I'm sick of you, Dad, and your stupid oversize car."

My mother was the one who loved that Lincoln. She was
still healthy in those years, but she had varicose veins, so
she liked to keep her legs elevated in the backseat. That
car was so big she could stretch out like a sedan queen.
I thought it was the height of vulgarity to have such a
big car (this was before SUVs). Every time Dad tried to
park it—or, as I used to say, dock it—I was mortified. I
was downwardly aspirational back then, into the importance of living simply (but attractively, of course). And
I tyrannized my parents with my inflexible taste, railing like a prophet against their music, shoes, and shampoo. This car was almost as bad as driving a Winnebago,
I thought.

With traffic passing on either side of us, Dad and I were
yelling, blood boiling.

"You're completely out of line, Bobby!"

"You're the one who's out of line! I don't need this! I don't need you!" I made him pull over, got out of the car, put my mother in the passenger seat, and sat in the back, the petulant child. I remained silent all the way to Westchester, where I boarded a commuter train to Manhattan without saying good-bye.

I didn't speak to him for months. I can't say I didn't feel an ache about being so cold and impenetrable. But nonengagement seemed the best solution back then. Now I wince at the off-putting cocktail of my pretentiousness and immaturity. My parents didn't deserve that from me. Never. All they wanted was for me to be happy.

"Sorry, Mom, I just don't have anything to say to him," I'd tell her when she called to try to mend things between my father and me.

"Sure you do," she told me. "You have no idea how much you have in common."

What we had in common was her, the last person in the world I wanted to hurt. And it pained her deeply to be in the middle of our fights. She took our feelings so seriously. Can a son just decide not to talk to his father? What does that do to a family?

"Maybe after a year, I'll feel better," I told her. "For now I need a break."

Bobby," she said. "I wish the two of you would grow up and accept each other."

At the time I couldn't imagine it. But maybe today, twenty years later, when we're driving north through New England once again, we'll have our bonding-buddy road trip. And maybe it will bring us to a scenic vista of reconciliation. He's in the passenger seat of my old Saab.

I'm the driver in charge, not him—that's a first. I like the feeling of control it brings me. His brown vinyl suitcase is in the back, bottle of Snapple in his hand. I hope it doesn't end up all over my car. Keeping one hand on the wheel, I pop in a tape I've carefully selected. He tries to like it, and almost does. But then he wants me to put on a baseball game. I refuse. He wants the air conditioner on high, and I tell him I can't stand the cold. Does he have to take every call on his phone? I don't want to listen to his banal conversations. All this, and we haven't even gotten out of Connecticut.

While merging from the Merritt Parkway to Route 95, I get an idea that might save this trip. It's based out of need as much as desperation. I pull out my pocket notebook and a pen, and hand them to him. Then I grab a folder with a file of song lyrics that need a lot of work before my first rehearsal Monday.

"Can I run them past you and see what you think?" I ask.

"Sure, I'd be delighted," he says.

Indeed, this is what he lives for. Solicited advice. It's rare I ask him anything, especially when it comes to writing. But that doesn't mean he doesn't have plenty to tell me. I sing him one of my songs from memory. He studies the lyrics on the page. "First off, what you've written is way too long," he tells me.

I begin to argue, then realize maybe he's right.

"Second, I can't really tell what this song is about."

"What do you mean?"

He answers astutely. Then, to my delight, a real collaboration begins. He starts jotting down ideas. Morris and Hammerstein? No. But we get so into it that we lose

track of everything but the work. The miles and hours
fall away as new lyrics, better than what I had before,
come together. He sings them to me, and I tweak them.
Before we know it we're pulling into our inn. It's a lovely
old clapboard place.

"Isn't that nice," says the assistant manger, "father and
son!"

"And he writes for travel magazines, so you might be
in luck," Dad chirps back.

The room, while clean and charming, doesn't have
views because he insisted I book ground floor so he
wouldn't have to climb any stairs. It also doesn't have the
elaborate cable TV choices he requires. But it has something very important to me—a living room with a pullout
couch. I cannot face the idea of sleeping right next to
him. I don't trust he won't snore all night. I don't trust
that I won't snore either. And there's this squeamishness
I feel around him when I see him with his shirt off in the
bathroom. Is that what I'm going to look like in thirty-five
years? Waking up right next to him in the morning would
be too intimate. So we share a space, but with extra space
between us.

On Sunday, Aunt Sylvia drives over from Rutland, Vermont. (She still drives at eighty-five, but only during the
day.) We go to lunch at a classy restaurant by a waterfall.
She's telling us about her trip to Italy with her fifty-six-
year-old bachelor son.

"We spent a few days in Positano," she says. "Our
hotel had a view of the Mediterranean. We had perfect
weather."

"Your trips always sound marvelous," Dad says.

He sounds wistful. Her son, my cousin Steve, takes

Aunt Sylvia on a big trip every year. I can't imagine that with my father. But then, my cousin is a devoted son, the type who calls constantly. And he and his mother are so aligned in taste and temperament that they are well-suited travelers. He selects destinations and hotels. Aunt Sylvia goes along happily. My father would never do that. He has his own ideas.

Under big birch trees shimmering in the summer sunlight, I sit across the table, drinking white wine and listening to brother and sister catch up. With my mother out of the picture, I can't help but notice what a pair of bookends they are. They have the same fine white hair and good olive skin. They are similarly shaped and sit back in their chairs the same way. Yes, their dispositions are different. He's relaxed, and she's tightly wound. He's Linus, she's Lucy. But despite their differences, they are extremely close. Well, they were orphans together. Big sister comforted little brother. She was there to mother him, throw him birthday parties, help with homework, and shop for clothes during his tender adolescence. He didn't have a father of his own to talk to about dating.

"And he was pretty shy as a teenager," she tells me. "Once when our grandmother arranged a date for him for a high school dance, your father said he had no desire to take the girl. It sounded so funny. Our grandmother told him desire had nothing to do with it."

I like hearing her talk about Dad's first years of dating. Maybe it will shed light on the romantic renaissance fair he's putting me through right now. Aunt Sylvia says that in his twenties, when he dated attractive women whom his friends also liked, my father just handed them over to them.

"He's always trying to make people happy," she says.

"Always?" I ask.

"Unless it gets in the way of his own fun, of course," she says, as she turns to Dad. "Remember that night in Palm Beach last winter when you stood me up, Joe?"

"All too well," he replies.

"What happened?" I ask.

"I had everything set out on the table for dinner, and he just never showed up," she says while Dad finishes her salmon. "I got worried and called the doorman and had people looking for him all over the building. I thought he had a stroke or something."

But then she looked outside and saw his car wasn't in the parking lot.

"I knew what happened. Edie had called him at the last minute, and your father just forgot about me," she says, as she gives him a nudge. "He'd done it to me once before with her. She called, and he vanished when we had plans. Imagine!"

"Love is a funny thing." Dad sighs as he chews his salad. "Also sadly fleeting."

"I think the whole thing is just ridiculous at your age," she clucks.

"So you never dated anyone after Uncle Dan passed away?" I ask her.

"Only once and I almost died. A man from my condo asked me to a concert at Tanglewood. I knew he was fond of me, but I didn't want any romantic involvement."

"Aunt Sylvia! Really! Was he cute?"

"Cute? Who's cute at eighty-five? He was a bright, well-dressed man, that's all."

"So did you go on the date?"

"I couldn't believe I said yes. But then, the night before, I got into a panic. I couldn't sleep. I had to take pills. I don't know why I didn't cancel."

"But you went? So what happened? Anything?"

"Not a thing. An hour before he was to pick me up I got a call. He'd had a minor heart attack that morning."

"Oh, my goodness," I say.

"And I hate to say it, but I was relieved," she says.

She shakes her head disapprovingly, then laughs at herself. Dad laughs, too.

I watch them across the table on a perfect Vermont afternoon, handsome senior citizens, both alone in the world now, with the loves of their lives gone. We are three single people, living on our own, sleeping in beds alone. Are we in the same boat? Not exactly. After all, they both have children who care about them. They have memories of raising families and happy marriages. They know what loving deeply means.

Meanwhile, I have Dad. We sit under the awning on the flagstone patio of the inn later, looking out at the mountains of central Vermont and working on my lyrics. Never mind that none of them will end up getting used in my show. Just for this moment we are happy with what we are doing. We find rhymes for this word, metaphors for that one. I don't know if I've ever enjoyed him as much as right now. With fingers that look like mine, he scribbles in a terrible scrawl that could be my own. We work into the late afternoon and beyond. Words fly down onto the page, then get crossed out, reworked. We recite. Rewrite. Argue, and then, deliciously, come to agree.

Hours pass. I look up from my lyrics and see, above

his head, fireflies. Beyond them, the sun is setting and the first star is rising over the farthest mountain ridge. Out on the pond across the road, a couple of unchecked bullfrogs compete with our singing.

It is a perfect and long-overdue moment.

# PART III

# Reconstructive Purgery

# CHAPTER 1

# New Year, New Hip

Now it's fall, and Yom Kippur is coming, the big day of atonement. A day for fasting and asking God forgiveness for sins. I guess Dad's conscience is clean because he's scheduled hip-replacement surgery. Yom Kippur, the holiest day of the year. I'm not devout either, but it seems reckless, taunting the almighty in this particular way.

Well, Mom was the one who cared about Judaism. But once we buried her, Dad headed right to the shrimp scampi and lobster rolls. Like a dog off a leash. Why not get the old hip replaced on Yom Kippur? In a Jewish area like Great Neck, he's telling me, there are plenty of openings for surgery that day. He figures if he can get it done in October, then he'll be back in Florida for the winter to run around like new.

"And, besides," he observes, "my doctor doesn't want me eating, so I'll be fasting anyway. You don't even need to be around. I can drive myself to the hospital and leave the car in long-term parking. I'll be fine. You don't have to worry at all."

Well, I do worry. His heart is not in the shape it should be for major surgery. And as annoying as he might be at times, I don't want to lose the old man. If he's gone, who's going to call me six times in an afternoon to change dinner plans? Who's going to push his cornucopia of pills on me with evangelical fervor each time I sneeze? Who's going to give me unsolicited advice about my career? Regale me with his bridge scores? Nag me to bring him my old socks because his are too tight? More important, who's going to be around to say, "It's a thrill to hear from you," each time I call, even if he's only half the listener my mother was? A hip replacement is serious at his age. I'm worried. I really should be there at dawn to take him to the hospital.

"I guess I could come out and spend the night," I say.

"That would be wonderful, a real mitzvah," he says.

So, on Yom Kippur Eve, while synagogues are filled with the pious and repentant, I go out to Great Neck to sleep over. At the Centra, he's waiting for me in the lobby, which is deserted at nine P.M. Only one other person is around, a lady in a hairnet, asleep in a lobby chair, with head down against her pink housedress. Dad's in an old sweatshirt. "I'm so glad you're here, Bobby," he tells me. "Just delighted." We pass an hour playing Scrabble. Then it's time to go to sleep. His foldout bed in his tiny guest room is broken and covered with files. So I sleep on the living room couch. Only I can't sleep, not at all. He's snoring away in the next room, a kind of high-pitched dolphin-like snore, and I'm lying awake, wondering if the surgery is a mistake. By his television, there's a videotape made by my brother (the archivist of the family, who has a fascination for our lineage that I don't share.) It's a compilation of our home movies. I pop it in and am shocked to see my father as a slim teenager at the ocean with his sister, and then frisking with my very young mother at a mountain lake. The color is washed out, but their vitality as a couple comes through brightly. Soon there are two babies, quickly toddlers, then awkward boys mugging for the camera on family vacations. Careful as they were with money, they took us every year to the Caribbean. We found out in later years my mother was scared of flying and didn't want to leave any orphans behind. So my brother and I were included and treated like welcome traveling companions. My father spent much of his time behind the camera, intent on preserving his family. His shots were long and lingering, trained on the three of us so that you could almost sense his pride. As I grew older, I'd get behind the camera. Here he is, playing tennis with Mom the year of her two-tone hairdo. Here he is kissing her at the hotel in St. Croix, where she got drunk on coconut daiquiris, the only time we'd ever seen her out of control, tipsy in heels and white cocktail dress on a pebbled path under the palms. Here they are, dancing at my brother's bar mitzvah, Dad with hilarious sideburns, Mom in mod attire of the day. Dad did well to give us the life we had. But he also did well for himself, and he intends to continue to do so until the end. A bum hip isn't going to get in the way of his fun. When the video ends, I lean back on the couch. He's still snoring in the next room. I lie awake, admiring how brave he is, how insistent he is on wanting to enjoy himself. He wants to live, love, walk without pain. And he's bucking the system to ensure it, at eighty. Good for my old man.

I wake him up at dawn. He's in a terrible mood because he can't eat anything. He can't even have tea. He hobbles into the bathroom and has his typical marathon in there. Impossible as this is to fathom, on the day of such potentially dangerous surgery, he is lingering, reading a bridge magazine. I find myself tapping my fingers, fuming. Then he puts on his worst shirt (missing button, stained) and throws his personal things into a plastic bag from Kmart. "Dad, come on," I say. "You're going to a good hospital. You might meet someone. Wear a nice shirt and pack your stuff in a better bag."

"What does it matter, Bobby?"

"It matters to *me*. Is it so wrong I care about your appearance?"

"You used to nag your mother like this all the time, and it wore her out."

I go to his closet, pull down a decent black shoulder bag, and repack for him. He changes into a blue button-down shirt, resentful as a huffy six-year-old.

"You should be grateful I'm here to tell you what's good for you, Dad."

"Okay. Okay, already. For Pete's sake."

"Don't get testy with me, Dad."

"Okay. But please let's just go!"

I dislike having to be the parent to this willful kid, and I fume in his car as I drive and he listens to the morning news at a volume that only increases my aggravation.

In the hospital, I wait with him in an empty lobby of

the special-surgery unit. It really is a quiet day here, as if it's Christmas. I can't believe I almost let him go through this alone. Hospitals are so intimidating. If I outlive my brother, I wonder to myself, will there be anyone around to see me through something like this? Dad is suddenly in such a cheerful mood, with strangers to charm. A slim blond nurse asks him to change into a hospital gown.

"Gladly," he says. Her name is Mary, he finds out.

"And I'm Joseph," he says. "We make a good team."

Two orderlies bring a gurney. They help him climb on. His gown flaps open to reveal his hairless legs and soft belly. He lies on his back with his hands behind his head, smiling, looking around, happy to be getting his way— having his hip fixed despite all the naysaying expert advice. The last I see him, he's being wheeled down the hall while singing "Bye Bye Blackbird." Then he disappears through two swinging doors. Gone.

It's a six-hour operation. So I go find a synagogue to kill some time. What else do you do in Great Neck on Yom Kippur? I choose a modern-looking temple on Middle Neck Road and have to explain myself at the door because I'm a stranger without a ticket. But I get in. I put on a skullcap and prayer shawl and stand in the back of the sanctuary, feeling underdressed without a sports coat, watching all the families, husbands and wives, so scrubbed and attractive. People my age already have teenagers. I see good-looking fathers who could be my peers with arms around good-looking kids.

It's reminding me of all those years sitting with my parents in synagogue, far into my middle age, when my brother had to be with his wife's family in New Jersey. I'd watch all the people I knew from my Hebrew school days. Their lives had changed—marriages, mortgages, children. Mine had not. I was still Bobby, the bachelor son.

Dad would fall asleep during the sermons. Mom sat upright, focused on what small wisdoms a small-town rabbi could provide on a day for reflection. Sometimes she would take my hand and squeeze it. I'd often think she was naive, taking faith so seriously. It made her righteous, too. And she could make it hard for friends and relatives who dared to date outside the fold. To her, marrying a gentile was a crime as severe as armed robbery. It made dating hard for my brother, who was so shy. And when I had a lovely Catholic girlfriend my senior year of high school, I had to face Mom's petty disappointment on a daily basis. But synagogue was her succor. Year after year I'd sit with her there and sigh and roll my eyes as we'd rise and sit, rise and sit, for prayers that were achingly redundant. Later, when she was ill, and so frail, I'd be glad she had had the opportunity to pray for a better year. And at the end of the service there was always a big hug and kiss on the cheek as she'd wish me a good year, with the natural warmth of the one person who cared more than anyone. "Thank you for coming home," she'd always say. "It means the world to me." Then, outside on the marble steps above Clinton Avenue, after Dad's endless shmoozing, we'd head home to her matzoh ball soup.

Yizkor is a section of the service for the deceased. In Great Neck, now, I am alone, praying in memory of my mother. I imagine I am one of many in this synagogue with powerful memories of a parent's love, and regrets about the conflicts we had. Are regrets about conflicts all I'm going to have with my father? I can't get the thought out of my head now, while saying prayers in memory of my mother, that my father may not make it through his surgery today.

Soon, we get to the atonement prayer that's a main attraction on Yom Kippur. It's called the "Vidui" and starts with the word *Ashamnu*. The congregation rises, looking repentant. The traditional ritual prescribes that you chant your sins aloud and ask God forgiveness as you beat your breast. It's dramatic and soulful, the perfect way for expressing remorse for the litany of bad behavior that is my daily life.

*We abuse*
*We betray*
*We are cruel*
*We embitter*
*We falsify*
*We gossip. We hate. We insult.*

I'm thinking that "we" also judge people by their shoes, don't return calls from people who can't do anything for us, and give chatty fathers the bum's rush on the phone. The prayer is going on, becoming more intense now, as the congregation calls out more sins. I chant with them, beating my breast harder, faster now, with something like desperation.

*We resent!*
*We envy!*
*We mock!*
*We judge people for things that are beyond their control!*

I stop short. *Yes, I do*, I tell myself. *I do. I judge people. I judge all the time!* And it is as unkind as it is limiting.

On my way back to the hospital after services, I feel, if not purged, then at least chastened. Nothing like a breast-beating for some perspective, if only for a day. Yes, I am too judgmental. Too critical. And stuck. So I tell myself that, starting today, I am going to make a real effort to stop judging my father, along with everyone else.

A half hour later, I'm walking into North Shore Hospital. In a sunlit room in a cheerfully painted wing, I find Dad, rosy cheeked and singing. Jeff, my brother, is there, just arrived from holidays with his in-laws. We can't believe it. Is this how a man with a pronounced heart ailment behaves after going through the major hip-replacement surgery he had been warned against by experts?

"Well, look who's here," he says to a nurse. "It's son number two, Bobby!"

I'm so overwrought with delight at his condition that I can hardly force words out as I kiss his smooth forehead. "How are you doing, Dad? You look great."

"Everything went beautifully," he croons. "I couldn't be better."

Jeff and I give each other looks. We've been giving each other looks about my father ever since we were old enough to be cynical. Tonight, along with our relief and gratitude to still have him around, we are feeling only amusement. Dad loves his epidural. Loves his nurse and our attention. We're smiling at him in a way we rarely do in hospitals—smiles of happy surprise at a happy ending.

With Mom, hospital visits were never like this. We knew she'd never get better. I always felt guilty for feeling inconvenienced and not spending as much time with her as Jeff did, especially because he was the one with the family and the business to run. And I didn't know how to advocate for her if she wasn't getting the best treatment. But when Jeff sensed any doctor wasn't on top of things he got pushy and belligerent. Mom's blood condition—called polycythemia vera—was rare, and he knew more about it than many doctors. It made Dad and me feel useless and inadequate. He'd throw questions at staffs, demand answers, and get them. He had many hostile exchanges with arrogant and misinformed doctors. In hospitals he could be like a raging bull who would do anything necessary to see that attention was properly paid to our mother. And he demanded it from my father and me, too, which caused brutal tension between us.

One day, when my mother had been in our local Long Island hospital for more than a week, I strolled in late for an afternoon visit. Mom was asleep.

"Where have you been?" Jeff asked me.

"I went to the beach," I said.

"All afternoon?"

"I needed a break from this hospital. What's the problem?"

"I just got here to find you gone and Dad playing tennis. Mom was alone all day."

His nostrils were flaring, and his face was flushed, a kind of righteous Jewish Holy Roller look in his eyes. I knew he was right—I shouldn't have played hospital hooky when Mom was alone all day, trying so hard not to feel frightened. But I hated having him as the family gatekeeper and scorekeeper. Such a pushy conscience.

"I need you to get your ass in here when you say you'll be here," he said.

"I need you to stop telling me what to do," I shot back. "You're driving all of us crazy."

He sighed and lowered his voice. He looked exhausted, overwhelmed to be carrying the ball for Dad and me. "Don't you know what you do for her?" he said. "You're the one who entertains her. You make her laugh. Don't make me tell you how important that is. It's your only job here, and you better damn well do it."

He was right, of course, but it took me years to understand it fully. And by the time I did, she was dying, without her wits about her. By then all there was to do was sing to her and wait for the morphine to take her down and out, until her life had left her.

But now, today, tra la, there's this happy, snappy little hip-replacement miracle in which our Wonder Dad, so up for a good time, has pulled through with rosy cheeks and broad painkiller smile.

I feel tears. My brother is teary-eyed, too. It's for joy, and we shake our heads, amazed. Dad made it. He's going to be running around with more ease than before.

And then, because we suspect he'd do the same to us, we decide to ditch him. He'll be fine, we can see, and we go to dinner at a snooty French restaurant in upscale Manhasset, exactly the kind of place with genteel decor, uppity waiters, and overpriced entrées (no sharing plates) that Dad would hate. I'm glad to be out of the hospital and grateful my brother is easing up on the dutiful-son routine tonight. It's especially gratifying to play hospital hooky together on this, the end of the holiest day of the

Jewish year, and in what might be the most Episcopalian restaurant on Long Island.

"It was great you could spend the night and get him to the hospital today," he says.

"Seemed like a good idea," I say.

"He told me it meant the world to him that you wanted to be there."

"Unusually selfless of me, I guess," I say.

"Not unusual at all. You've been great. You're a great son."

I blush with pride at the acknowledgment.

The following day, we're visiting Dad again, when a wide-hipped peroxide blonde runs into his room in a high state of alarm. "Oh my God! Joey! You're alive! Thank God!" She's wearing brown lipstick and mascara, tight black slacks, a turtleneck, and a little white fur coat. Her name is Mini. She is anything but. And she is shrieking.

"I really thought you were dead, Joey!"

"I don't understand," he says.

"The security guard in your building told me you died in this hospital."

"What made him say such a thing?"

"It was a terrible misunderstanding," she says, as she fans herself with her hand.

"I'll say," he says.

"But that's what he told me when I went to wish you a happy holiday. So I got very upset and spread the word. So now your entire building thinks you're dead. It's a national day of mourning at the Centra, Joey."

"That's very flattering," he says.

"I better get back over there to tell everyone that you're

still alive. Everyone loves you so much, Joey. They'll be thrilled. See you soon!"

Then she leaves, leaving my brother and me in a cloud of eau de something or other.

"Who was that, Dad?" my brother asks.

"Mini," he says. "Just friends, nothing serious."

A moment passes. It's a little awkward, but nothing out of the ordinary.

Later, in the hospital parking lot, my brother tells me, "Mom was right. Life with him may be irritating, but it's never dull."

## CHAPTER 2

# Rehab Horribilis

n a week, he's over in rehab. But even though his new hip is going to be fine, he's depressed. He's not a patient patient, and six weeks of recovery time looms over him the same way it would for a little boy—he can't imagine taking that long to get back on his feet, and he's not interested in being stuck in a routine that isn't his own. To me, the rehab facility is kind of fabulous. It's in Manhasset, surrounded by woods, a low-rise brick design that could almost be Scandinavian. And at a time when celebrities are in and out of one kind of facility or another, the word *rehab* has a glamorous connotation. I wonder who else is in rehab with him. Maybe an elderly socialite or two?

"This place is surprisingly nice, isn't it?" I chirp.

I go out to see him often. To my dismay, he isn't getting many visitors. He doesn't like seeing friends when he isn't at his best, he tells me. What he needs is a wife to fuss over him all day long, bring him chicken soup, arrange his bedside table, do crosswords with him. He's bored. He spends hours watching TV, looking forward to visits from my brother, sister-in-law, their children, and guilty, guilty me. I'm busy in the city, working on revisions for an upcoming reading of a solo show, as well as a treatment I've been invited to pitch to a network. I am struggling to find a national audience. Meanwhile, I have become Dad's private entertainment.

Today, a week into his rehab, I am committed to getting a smile out of him. He's in a wheelchair in his room in a flannel shirt, with smudged glasses crooked on his nose. His mouth is turned down in a way that's unfamiliar to me. He's usually so sunny.

"Okay, ready for a joke, Dad?"

"Not in the mood," he says.

"Oh, come on. Since when do you turn down a joke?"

"Okay, fine. Go ahead," he says.

I pull my chair up close to make sure he's paying attention.

*So two young woman and one old woman are sitting in a sauna. There's a beeping sound. The first young woman presses her forearm, and the beeping stops. The others look at her with raised eyebrows. "That was my pager," she says. "I have a microchip under the skin of my arm." A few minutes later, a phone rings. The second young woman lifts her palm to her ear. When she finishes, she explains, "That was my mobile phone. I have a microchip in my hand." Now the older woman is suddenly feeling very low tech and out of it. But not to be outdone, she leaves the sauna, then returns with a piece of toilet paper hanging from her rear end.* "Well, would you look at that," she says. "I must be getting a fax!"

Dad doesn't laugh.

"Get it?"

"Yes, I get it."

"You don't think it's funny?"

"Eh," he says. "It's a little demeaning."

"To who?"

"'Who do you think? The elderly. We're not that ridiculous."

Maybe he's right. But that furrowed brow, weary voice of the dying—I have to turn his spirits around. Outside his window, the October leaves are gold and red, sifting in the afternoon air. He's in the autumn of his life. I'm no spring chicken either. But I refuse to accept that this is how it has to be with him for the next five weeks.

"You know what, Dad? Let's get you in a sweater. If you're going to sit around depressed, let's take it outside."

"No, I don't want to go outside."

"Why not?"

"It's too cold."

"You have no idea what the temperature is. It's a beautiful day, and if I schlep out here from the city, the least you can do is let me get some fresh air. Here's your sweater. I'll help you put it on." I grab his beige pullover from a shelf and try to drape it over him. He refuses it, like a willful two-year-old, pushing it back at me.

"Come on, Dad!"

"Bobby, please don't nag me. You want to come and visit, that's great, but I don't want to be forced to do anything. I'd rather be left alone."

He turns his attention to his TV. I let out a sigh.

"So that's it, Dad? We're going to have to spend the morning watching TV?"

"You can change the channel if you like."

"No, I think I'll just go home."

"You just got here."

"Well, it's an incredibly busy week for me."

His face lights up for the first time since I arrived. My career is his career.

"So what's cooking? Got a good assignment?"

"No, I told you what I'm doing. We're staging another reading of my show. And I'm pitching a TV show in L.A. next week."

The smile vanishes. He shrugs, makes a face as if he's just tasted sour milk.

"I'm excited, Dad. But you don't look pleased."

"You've been trying to get that show off the ground for two years. I hate to see you set yourself up for more disappointment."

"Pardon me?"

"I just think that this pie-in-the-sky stuff is going to give you nothing but heartache. Are they paying your way to California for the TV meeting?"

"Um. No. But it's a big deal to be invited."

"Big waste of your money, mark my words."

Irritation is bubbling up in me now, along with self-doubt I would rather ignore. A couple months ago we were gleefully writing songs together in Vermont. Why all this negativity now? He's in a bad mood. Nothing seems hopeful to him at the moment. And like me, he's too self-involved to check himself.

"I just hate to see you do things you don't get paid for, Bobby."

Why does he think I need his approval? He's never done anything that would make his advice worthy. I mean, what was his career? He rose all the way from Bay Shore real estate lawyer to administrative law judge for the New York State Department of Motor Vehicles, an appointment that allowed him to proudly refer to himself for the rest of his life as *Judge* Joseph Morris. He was no Thurgood Marshall. When I was in my twenties, failing at getting a career started and living at home, he used to come back from work and bore me at dinner with lackluster accounts of his day. The case of some poor schmuck who accidentally ran over the neighbor's dog. Drunk-driving adolescents. Speeding arrests in parking lots. Moving violations that were anything but moving. Dad kept asking me to come to court so I could see him on his elevated throne of justice, judging traffic criminals. "You'd be very intrigued," he told me. "And it would make a great TV series. If you write it, I'll sign on as an adviser." I'd snicker. What did he know? Now, twenty-five years after I rejected his dream, here he is rejecting mine.

"All I'm saying, Bobby, is that you should stick to what you're good at."

"I don't want to keep doing journalism for the rest of my life," I whine.

"You have nothing to be ashamed of when it comes to work. You're clever, and you've mastered a certain kind of writing. You get paid to write for a prominent publication that millions of people read."

"Except you, Dad."

"You know that I don't like the politics of that paper."

"Is it so wrong to want more from my career? I need to feel hopeful right now."

"Fine. But when it doesn't work out, remember who told you so."

I bolt up from my chair and push it into his bed so it clatters.

"Okay, Dad. I've heard enough. I'm going to go. I've got a busy week."

"As you like. Thanks for coming." He extends an arm to me as he always does for a hug. I ignore it and give him a cool pat on the shoulder instead, then storm out. Driving home, stuck in traffic, as I so often am on my tedious trips to him, I seethe.

"He's just frustrated, don't pay attention," my brother tells me later.

"I really can't stand him sometimes," I say. "I don't know why I visit."

"Because you know he loves his visits with you more than anything."

"We're always fighting. We drive each other crazy."

"That's not what I hear. He's always thrilled to see you."

"He loves when you bring your kids," I say. "He loves watching sports on TV with Ian. To him that's a perfect visit with a perfect grandson."

"Maybe. But it's not the same as you. Don't you know how much he adores you? He thinks of you as his soul mate."

"He does not."

"Yes, he does. He's always telling me how much he identifies with everything you do. You're doing everything he wishes he could have done with his own life."

"And what are you, Jeff? Chopped liver?"

"He loves me, he loves my family. But he is thrilled by you."

"Do you think he senses you're angry at the way he treated Mom?"

"Maybe. But I'm not as angry as I used to be."

I'm glad about that. For all of us. And I guess I could be flattered. My father thinks I'm a thrill. Don't some sons fight their whole lives to get that kind of reaction from their fathers? Instead, I just feel guilty that in a few days I have to leave him for a week to go to L.A. So, upset as I am with him, I drive out for another visit, leaving all kinds of work behind on my desk. He's still wallowing in depression, slumped in his wheelchair in his room, and devoid of the wonderful willful vitality that has always defined him. But I have a plan today. I know he still has it in him to sing. Without letting him argue, I wheel him outside into the warm autumn afternoon. I place him in front of a bench, and I sit down and get out my ukulele. The birds are almost shrill. I strum hard.

*I want to be happy*
*But I won't be happy*
*Till I make you happy too . . .*

Am I seeing the trace of a smile? The lines on his forehead relax, and his eyebrows descend, and his face goes from showing consternation to contentment to enjoyment. Then I see him start to speak the lyrics. I do want to make him happy. It's all I want.

But the happiness doesn't last long. When I wheel him back inside, I can't get him to show any enthusiasm for anything. I wonder if he is getting a look at his future and doesn't like what he's seeing, confined, controlled, dependent. He is eighty-one, now, after all. Even with a new hip, how much longer will he be able to frolic, flirt, run around from bridge games to concerts and salad bar restaurants?

One evening, when I'm back from L.A., I'm wheeling him into dinner at a long table with the other hip patients. (And I don't mean *hip* in the downtown sense of the word.) They are all in wheelchairs, which doesn't make for the most delicate dining. All women, mostly in their seventies, nicely dressed in muted colors, decent jewelry, well-tied scarves. Hip-replacement surgery is elective, and therefore selective—just the demographic I'm looking for, for him. A match! Why hadn't I thought of this before? A rehab romance, in-house and short-term, could be just the thing to cheer him up, put a little fizz in his day, set me free from worrying. Fifth Avenue Florence won't have to know. This could be a little starter course before he starts up with her for real in Florida. I can't help noticing that all the woman at his table look like pretty classy birds. And some of them are eyeing him like the cutest little worm they've ever seen. That ash blonde at the end of the table with excellent manners would be very attractive accessorized with something other than an IV pole. But Dad, who is usually so flirtatious, is paying no attention, even as they try to engage him in chatter.

"We didn't see you at bingo this morning, Joe," one says.

"Have you gotten an absentee ballot for the election?" another says. "It's less than a month away, and you're staying here through mid-November, right?"

"Yes, I'm aware," he says. "You don't have to remind me."

He eats his dinner in a sullen daze. I don't understand

this at all. He's got a new hip, a new life ahead, Fifth Avenue Florence in Florida, and plenty of good fishing for affection right here, right now. How can my Love Pelican be letting all these lovely lady fish get away? "Dad," I say, as I wheel him back to his room after lunch, "those women at your table look really nice. Have you seen any husbands around?"

"Not one. I think they're all widowed."

"So why don't you chat with them a little more?"

"What do I have to chat about?"

"Anything. Or you could ask one to join you for the movie tonight."

"No, Bobby, I don't think so."

"What about seeing if any of them are bridge players?"

"Playing bridge with four wheelchairs at a table is a physical impossibility. I tried it once, and it was like the Mad Hatter's tea party."

We're halfway to his room and another attractive lady— wearing pearls and a small Star of David—is wheeled past us. She says hello. Her eyes are a lovely shade of blue, just like my mother's. "And how are *you* this evening?" I ask.

"Better every day," she replies.

"How much longer will you be here?"

"Another four weeks, I'm told," she says.

"Oh! Dad! That's the same as you, isn't it?"

"Don't remind me," he says.

He won't perk up. And after a few more niceties, she excuses herself and disappears down the hall. I wheel him back to his room. "Okay, now *she* was exactly your type," I say. "Why don't you ask if she'd like to have lunch with you tomorrow?"

"No, not now, thanks."

"Why not?"

"I don't feel like socializing."

"Okay, you know what? I'll go ask her for you. You have four weeks to get to know each other. You've already wasted too much time. I'll be right back!"

He brings his hand down firmly against his wheelchair.

"Bobby, please!" he yells. "Leave it alone already!"

I freeze right over him, a looming shadow with an agenda. I should recognize that all he needs right now is my hand and some affection. Instead, I want to fix him. I just can't stand to see him so resigned to wallowing in his loneliness, so not himself.

"Leave it alone? Leave it alone? Sure I can leave it alone, Dad. But let me tell you something. I have a date tonight. And I have to get going or I'll be late. And if you want me to enjoy myself, then I need you up and dating, too. So tomorrow I want you to brush your hair, put on a clean shirt, and make nice to the ladies with the good jewelry. Right now, I've got to go. Tonight, you can date vicariously through me!"

For the first time all night, he sits up straight and looks me in the eye.

"Good luck, Bobby," he says as he waves. "I wish you all the luck in the world."

"Thanks," I say. "I'll need it."

Mercifully, traffic isn't bad, and I get to the city just in time to make it to a midtown bar to meet up with a guy called Guy. But he isn't here yet. I sit down and order a martini. We met a couple months before but have not been able to connect since.

He's a half hour late now.

I order another drink and look around the dimly lit bar. This place, it's so predictably groovy—gay-century modern with the big globe lights and Eames knock-off coffee tables. And all the men in here are thirty years old. Or trying to look it. None of them have anything resembling my middle-aged paunch. All of them have flawless skin and boyish hair without even a fleck of gray. And why are they all wearing long-sleeve T-shirts under short-sleeve ones? They're all laughing shrilly and drinking the new muddled mint martini with artisanal vodka from Chechnya. I feel old in my collared shirt. But then again, if eighty is the new seventy, then forty is the new thirty, right? That makes me, what? Thirty-five? Nobody wants to act or dress his age anymore. Why shouldn't I be here, trying to fit in with all these skinny twenty-somethings in low-riding jeans?

But where is my date? It's embarrassing to be alone here. Am I being stood up? I could have been spending this time with my father. I hated having to rush off from him tonight, when he's so down. I check my cell phone. No messages. Why am I sticking around this bar? Am I so desperate? Another drink. This music—house music or whatever it is. It's so monotonous, and it's pounding away, reminding me of all the years I've stood around at bars like this one, snubbing or being snubbed. How many more years will I be holding a drink in my hand, staring into space, hoping to make a connection, nodding my head to this monotonous music I hate? All I'd really like to hear right now is one of the sweet, uplifting sentimental songs that my father loves so much.

I'm drunk when Guy finally arrives. He's looking handsome, and tells me he's sorry to be so late. He was stuck at dinner with the president of a big jewelry company, he explains, or something like that. Name-dropping. I'm not impressed.

"I blew my father off so I could be here on time to meet you," I tell him.

"I'm sorry. I didn't have my cell phone, so I couldn't call."

"You're almost an hour late! Do you know that?"

"Can you lower your voice? You're making a scene."

"Whatever." I slam down my drink and storm outside into the cool autumn night. I assume he's going to follow me, but he doesn't. It's pathetic, but I can't quite make myself go home. Moments later, he comes outside, steps up to me, lights a cigarette.

"Sorry," I say. "It's been hard with my dad."

I assume he's going to ask me about him, show some concern, let me get it off my chest so we can reconcile.

"Look," he says. "I don't think this is going to work out tonight."

"You know," I say, "I've never known why it's so hard to get together with you."

"It's been a busy time," he says. "But I'll call you. I definitely will." He throws his cigarette on the sidewalk and goes inside. I let my shoulders drop and feel the air let out of my night with a whoosh. Then, after a long sigh, I head home.

CHAPTER 3

# Back in His Saddle

My TV show doesn't sell. My staged reading ends
up getting no backers. I don't tell my father any of
this because it will prove he was right. That would
be intolerable.

Meanwhile, Dad's life has moved on beautifully.
Against everyone's advice, he gets himself out of rehab
early and goes home to his assisted-living place in Great
Neck, where he recuperates ahead of schedule. Then
he packs his things, and, with a brand-new hip, he hobbles onto the free flight he booked on his miles account
months ago, and soars right back down to Florida, where
he is happiest.

And much to my delight, he quickly finds his *she*-legs
again and takes up where he had left off last summer

with—ta da!—Fifth Avenue Florence. It gets off to a funky start when he shows up an hour early to pick her up for a date. She's in her bathrobe, but it doesn't faze her, nor do any of his other habits that I thought would be deal breakers—including his urge to defend his beloved Republican Party to all her liberal friends. Apparently she likes having him around as more than a bridge partner. She's taking him to lunch at the Palm Beach Country Club, a scene far beyond his social sphere.

"It's a gorgeous place, Bobby," he tells me on one of his phone dispatches. "And Florence is a very classy lady. A woman of the world. You'd approve."

"So has there been any canoodling yet, Dad?"

"Canoodling? Is that like cuddling?"

"With benefits. Although I don't know why I'm asking."

"For now I think she just likes having an escort, but I'm willing to be patient."

"So tell me more about her, Dad. Looks?"

"Fair. Nice figure. And she's younger than me by ten years."

"Sounds perfect."

"Well, she's also a little self-centered and domineering."

"Oh. In what way?"

"She likes to decide the agenda when we go out. And she tends to be more interested in spending time with her friends than with mine."

"Well, you love meeting new people, so that's good, right?"

"Most of her friends aren't anything extra. But then,

none of the women down here are all that pleasant, especially the bridge players. They always find something to complain about. Some of them have chips on their shoulders the size of matzoh balls. You can tell a lot about a woman by the way she plays bridge."

"And Florence is *great* at bridge, right, Dad?"

"Yes, she's a good player, but she's very strong-minded, so it can be a little hard to take. I don't like being henpecked. I like to keep things easy."

"Oh, come on, Dad, she must be very fond of you if she's asking you out so much. I think it's time to take it to the next level."

"The thought has crossed my mind. But how? If I ask her out to a movie and I take her hand and she pulls it away, do I have to apologize for being too forward?"

"No. Pretend it never happened."

"And if I want to kiss her, where is the best place to give it a try?"

"How about at her front door when you drop her off after the next date?"

"I don't escort her to her door. My hip's still recuperating."

"How about in the car? You're keeping it clean for her, aren't you?"

"I'm trying to keep things off the passenger seat."

"So you have some of your music playing, maybe Frank Sinatra, very smooth, and then you just kind of lean over and kiss her good night and see where it leads."

He says he'll give it some thought. But he's still a little leery, I can tell.

I can't say I blame him. And besides, what do I know about putting the moves on anybody? When I hang up the phone, my face is flushed with excitement, as if I'm the one about to kiss someone good night. Why am I so desperate for him to pursue a relationship with this Fifth Avenue Florence? Is it zip-code envy?

Am I social climbing through my father?

## CHAPTER 4

# Demolition Dating

One Friday night in December, a few weeks after Dad's departure for Florida, when I'm in the city with no plans for the weekend (even as my old man is booked nonstop), I find myself pulled into an intense little e-mail correspondence with a guy on my dating Web site. We parry over a bestselling novel I like. He suggests it's overwritten. I disagree. I rave about Moby's new CD. He dismisses it. We only know each other's Internet names (his is particularly pretentious—an arcane Danish modern furniture designer), but after a few hours of e-mailing back and forth, we have gotten to level two and exchanged phone numbers. I take a breath and call him to arrange a dinner date.

He picks up his phone and says, "Not that Bob Morris!" He has my name on his caller ID. It throws me. He knows

of me, and I know of him. He's a book agent. We set up a
date for the next night, but it bothers me that we know
of each other. I like to keep my dating life private. That
way, when it doesn't work out, I don't have to worry about
word getting around. Repercussions and reverberations.

I choose my outfit carefully on Saturday night. Leather
pants and a pleated shirt. Very avant-garde, I think. My
cheeks are burning from the cold when I walk into a
downtown restaurant. I'm anxious. Part of me is already
trying to think of a nice way to make it just drinks rather
than dinner. The restaurant is noisy, everyone with a cell
phone and BlackBerry at the ready so they don't have to
commit fully to being where they are. I don't see anyone
I know, and that's a huge relief. I hate introducing dates
to friends. So awkward. Is that him at the bar, face glowing in the light?

"Ira?"

"Bob?"

We shake hands and sit down at a corner table. I order
a vanilla martini. He orders a Diet Coke. He's handsome, but I think he kind of looks like me. And I am not
my type. He's small, with wavy salt-and-pepper hair—a
Jewish Richard Gere is how people might see him. Edgy
tortoiseshell glasses. Brown eyes. Good skin. Strong-
looking hands. Bold yellow turtleneck sweater that only a
very confident man in his early forties could pull off. Attitude to spare. And that voice. How do I describe it? It's
definitely New York, but with an almost plummy English
overlay that doesn't quite erase his nasal Bronx accent.

I don't know anybody from the Bronx. It's enough that
I still know people from the Islips, where I'm from. This
is only one of many toxic thoughts I bring to the table.

(And later I find out that he almost writes me off for my leather pants and vanilla martini.) But there is an instant rapport. We are both so opinionated.

"I can't stand how gentrified this neighborhood is," he says about the West Village, where I'm proud to have a rent-stabilized apartment among the wealthy.

"Doesn't bother me at all," I say. "In fact, it feels validating to have an Olsen twin living around the corner."

"The whole city I knew as a kid is gone," he says.

"Which means there are no more heroin addicts?"

"Yes, but now we have fashion editors," he says.

We shouldn't laugh, but we do. Maybe two abrasive personalities are better than one. Neither of us seems to see the need to be careful. Our conversation is the least-strained first-date conversation I've ever had. We argue about books and movies and magazines. We gossip about people we have in common. I feel so comfortable with him that I let down my guard and do something I would never do on a first date: I talk a little about my father and his dating travails. Instead of changing the subject (could there be any less-attractive subject on a first date?), Ira just listens and laughs. He appreciates that I'm concerned about my old man, and then he tells me that his mother is a widow, too, and in Great Neck, no less. My ears go up like a dog who has just heard the food hit the bowl. "Hey! My father lives in Great Neck!"

"Oh yeah? Where?"

"The Centra, assisted living."

"I know that building very well."

"So what's your mother like? How old is she? Is she attractive?"

He describes her as a small, youthful eighty-two-year-old with a big SUV. She still drives, runs around to her senior groups and lectures—an upbeat, lively woman. Okay, she's a finger-wagging socialist who has no interest in involving herself with another man. No matter. She could be good for my father, I'm thinking, especially if Florence fails. Someone for the spring, when he's back from Florida. Ira dismisses me with a brush of his hand. He's tough.

"Why don't we table this topic for now?" he says.

"Why? Just ask your mom if she'd be up for meeting him!"

"Maybe I should have brought her along on this date," he says.

As we eat our meal and then pay the bill—Dutch—I realize that the hour has sped by. This man with the name that makes me cringe could easily be a friend.

But boyfriends?

He's kind of affected, if not a little flamboyant. And I mean, not to harp on it, but come on—Ira Silverberg. Can I date such a Jewish-sounding name? With cold wind on our cheeks and clouds of condensation coming out of our mouths, we walk through the Village after dinner, chatting away, with endless topics to cover and more still untouched. I should not have had that last martini. He had only Diet Cokes. And okay, I'm not on my best behavior because I'm not intimidated by him, or even concerned that I'm making a good impression. He isn't quickening my heart the way a good date should. But what the hell? It's cold. He's cute. Or cute enough. Outside my building, with take-out menus swirling around our feet, I kiss him good night. He doesn't pull away. But he also doesn't egg me on for more. He just smiles. He has a slightly crooked tooth. His eyes are squinty, and if they're pools, only lap pools. They're also brown when I prefer blue. But they are full of light and life. "Good night," he says. "Let's do it again."

He walks away in a chic black shearling coat, all posture and dignity.

Amusing guy. And compelling on a level that isn't superficial.

On our second date, I meet the dog. I have come to pick Ira up in his Soho apartment. The place is a well-designed walkup with midcentury furniture in bold colors. Most impressive are his shelves of books. Books by friends. Books he published, edited, sold as an agent. On the one hand he's a flip city boy into clothes and design. But on the other hand, there are all these books he is absolutely passionate about, that he championed, and I'm impressed. His heart is in the world of serious authors and artists. There are black-and-white photographs of him as a teenager hanging around with William Burroughs and Allen Ginsberg. This Ira Silverberg of the Bronx has lived three times as many lives as I have. He was even a doorman at Limelight, the nightclub. He's younger than me by five years. Yet he knows so much more than I do.

The only thing he doesn't know, apparently, is how to control his dog, Byron, a high-strung cairn terrier. As we are leaving his apartment to go to a holiday party, I am putting on my coat when I feel something at my ankles, and I jump when I look down. This little dark cloud of fur is trying to sink his teeth into me to keep me from leaving.

"Hey! Your dog's biting my legs!"

"Byron! No!" Ira says as he pulls him away. The dog

tries to snap at him. It is an alarming display of domestic doggy discord. In fact, it's rather like seeing that the child of someone you're dating is an out-of-control hellion. What to think about it?

After he locks his front door, he tells me, "Byron has abandonment issues."

"Meaning he doesn't like to be left?"

"Exactly."

"Does he bite a lot of people?"

"Not enough, if you ask me. This neighborhood is overrun with tourists."

I laugh. We laugh the whole night, and he's great at the party I've been invited to. Even though it's more a style crowd than a literary one, he knows people and fits right in. He's witty and attractive, animated to the point of antic. But then, a little while into the evening, I start to worry that he's talking way too loud. And I wish that his Bronx accent wasn't quite so pronounced. I find myself fighting the impulse to interrupt what he's saying to people—isn't he going on a bit too long? Of course, everyone is finding him wonderful. I rarely have dates who fit right into my pushy little party world. At the end of the evening, he asks if I'll walk Byron with him.

"Is he going to be biting anyone?" I say.

"Only men in bad shoes," he says.

So on a cold December night—our second date—we walk Byron together, his little Toto dog, whose tail is wagging sweetly as he pulls Ira on his leash past the well-dressed evening-outers on the streets of Soho. The dog is twelve years old.

"But he has puppy energy," Ira says.

Puppy energy. I like that, it's a kind of adorable, straining-at-the-leash quality, a quality I am seeing in Ira, too. For better and for worse, he is nothing if not high-strung.

When it comes time for our third date the next weekend, I am very anxious.

I dress carefully, in a black cashmere turtleneck that will hide my love handles. I shave twice. I can't really tell what he thinks of me, but I get the sense that we're both trying to make it work.

We're in his apartment. Bryon the dog is out of sight somewhere, giving us space to be alone. We finish the Japanese take-out dinner. Barry White is singing "Can't Get Enough of Your Love." We've got a shag-rug vibe going. I've had several drinks. He's had several cigarettes. The lights are low, candles flickering anxiously. All around us his book collection looms. All those brilliantly convoluted minds seem to be egging us on. It's better company than I'm used to. It's midnight in Soho, and, while the world outside is racing around in expensive jeans, looking for love or a good party, we have arrived at this, shoes off, the third date.

The night when sex has to happen.

And the disturbing truth is that, because I'm unsure of our chemistry, I have not been rushing to get into bed with Ira. Apparently Byron isn't all that eager for me to get into bed with Ira either. As I climb on in his candlelit bedroom, stomach in knots from the anxiety, the growling from underfoot that I've been ignoring suddenly becomes a fierce gray mass lunging at my bare feet. Grrr! Arf! The teeth just miss me as I jump, afraid for my life. "Byron," Ira yells as the little dog pulls back under the bed. "Bad dog! No!"

I'm in shock. What is it with me and dogs on dates? I laugh nervously at the unchecked feral energy attacking from under the bed. It's something between Dr. Freud and Dr. Seuss. Sex as the out-of-control animal with sharp teeth menacing in the night.

"He just attacked me! Why did he do that?"

"I'm so sorry," Ira says. "Cairns are cave dwellers, and when he lunges like that, he's just protecting his lair. It's not personal, just instinctual, something his breed does."

Eventually we turn out the lights.

I want to be physically responsive, in the moment. But I can't with my mind firing in so many directions. Do I really want to do this tonight? If I don't really feel this, how will I do this? It ends with all the sophistication of sixteen-year-olds in the backseat of a car.

"High school sex," I say, as I jump up and get dressed.

"Better than nothing," he replies, smiling from the bed.

"I have to go," I say.

"I'll call you."

"Okay," I say. Then I open the door and flee, letting it slam behind me.

Walking home past many lovely young couples, I flail my fist in the air.

"What is wrong with you?" I mutter. "Get over yourself!"

I know there's something very good in him, and I know he's the marrying kind, an unusual trait in New York men. He's a deep person. Funny. Handsome. Honest. Yet my impulse is to run. I always run. Why? Am I still afraid to become intimate with anyone, no matter how appropriate? By making a real effort to commit, am I making myself too vulnerable? Will I have to turn myself inside out in order to make this work? What if he decides I'm not good enough after a month? Maybe it just isn't meant to be. That happens between people all the time. I can't force it. He's wonderful. But he just isn't my type. He leaves a message the next morning. I don't call back.

I don't return an e-mail either. Is he figuring out that I'm pulling away? He's leaving for California for a week, he writes. I feel awful. We should talk.

But what is there to say? I'm too ashamed of myself to explain myself.

The next day, flowers arrive. He must have ordered them just before getting on his flight. They are white narcissi, delicate as they are fragrant.

There's a card inside. "If that was high school," it says, "then let's go to college."

I spend the week talking incessantly about Ira to my friends, saying he's so great and so good looking, but just not for me. "So I guess I'm letting it unravel," I tell Marisa.

"Are you out of your mind?" she says. "Don't you dare!"

It's Christmas Eve, and I'm having dinner with her family in New Jersey again. She is now completely entwined with Silvano, and they have become a flashy little It couple.

"But I just don't think I can make it work," I whine. "It's complicated."

Later, another friend, Amy, is dropping me off after dinner. She's divorced and finding the dating scene impossible.

"Why the hell would you dismiss a man like that?" she asks.

I try to explain that, while I like Ira, I don't think I'd like sleeping with him. She isn't buying it. "It's too early for you to decide if you're physically compatible or not," she says. "You have to sleep with a guy three times before you can make a good decision."

"But why? What will that prove if I don't like it the first time?"

"Three times," she says. "That's the rule. Promise you will before you give up."

I can't promise. I'm too afraid. And I don't want to extend myself only to be disappointed. And isn't there something to be said for not getting in deep with someone you are having doubts about? I don't want to hurt him when I run. God, this is so complicated. I don't do this! I have never known how to do this!

Christmas comes and goes, lonely and silent in the city. I know Ira's in town, but I don't call.

"It's just too much of a strain," I tell my friend Gillian. "I should move on, let it go."

"You've got to be kidding," Gillian says.

"It's just too complicated. I don't want to jerk him around and hurt him."

"He sounds like the person you've been searching for."

"I haven't been searching."

"Liar! You have so."

"But I've never wanted someone like him. I don't feel comfortable."

Gillian puts down her coffee cup and grabs my chin. She looks disgusted.

"You know something?" she says. "You have to stop thinking so much. And you have to stop being so critical. But mostly, you have to stop being afraid. You're afraid to return his affection. You're afraid to commit to really trying with someone who is actually right for you. You're afraid of everything, and it's ruining your life. Call him."

"Call him? When? Right now? Why?"

"Because I'm telling you to, that's why," she says.

"What am I supposed to say?"

"Tell him you're sorry you didn't return his calls and try to make another date."

I know I should. But I can't. I don't know why, but I can't.

"You're making the biggest mistake of your life," she says.

At the airport on my way to Florida the next day, I bump into a dog trainer I know. I don't know why, but I find myself telling her all about Byron, Ira's cairn terrier. She is shocked to hear about how he attacks from under the bed.

"But Ira says that cairns are cave dwellers," I explain enthusiastically. "So lunging from under the bed is typical because it's a characteristic of the breed, right?"

She looks at me as if I'm out of my mind. "Um, I don't know what dog books he's been reading," she says. "But bad behavior like that is not the breed. It's the dog."

I don't know why I find this so hilarious. All I know is that I want to call Ira and tell him, tease him, and hear him come up with the perfect response. I start to dial his number. Then I stop. I don't want to reengage. I don't have time. I am going to Palm Beach to see my father,

who is having problems with Fifth Avenue Florence. He
needs me, and I am hoping to forget my own emotional
fiasco so I can focus on his. And then I'm hoping I'll have
something to do, anything to do, when I get back for New
Year's Eve.

# CHAPTER 5

# Tawdry Palms

The flight to Palm Beach is on time, and within a few hours, I'm in the pleasant Florida sunshine in a rental car, a white Sebring convertible, cruising to Dad along I-95. The wind in my face is starting to blow thoughts of Ira right out of my head. Traffic is moving well. I'm playing with the radio when Dad calls. It's hard to hear him with the top down. But I get the gist. He's not so good. He's happy I'm coming to see him, of course. He can use cheering up, some "moral support," he says. He's thinking he has to end it with Fifth Avenue Florence. It just keeps getting worse.

"I can't believe it, Dad," I tell him. "She's taking you to the Palm Beach Country Club all the time. You told me you're compatible at the bridge table."

"But she's getting harder and harder to take, Bobby."

"Everybody has their flaws, Dad. Don't be so sensitive."

"Last night she suggested I was just filler until Mr. Right comes along."

"Dad, come on! She was joking. That's what people do when they're just getting comfortable with each other. They joke. You can't take it seriously."

"Then she told me I was only after her for her money."

"Again, joking! Don't you know that? What would you want with her money?"

"I just don't know what to say to her. She makes me feel second-rate. Do you know that last night she introduced me at a party as her walker?"

Ouch. That's a little much. "A walker? Really? Oh boy."

"At first I thought she meant someone to lean on, then I found out it's more like a gentleman you use as an accessory when you have to go out for the evening. "

"So what did people do when she called you her walker?"

"Oh, they laughed. But it hurt my feelings."

"Look, I swear to you, Dad, she was just joking."

"I'm not an extra man for her to drag around."

"Of course you aren't, Dad. And she didn't mean anything by it."

This is not good, and not at all what I had in mind for his new life. All the hard pimp work I've done on his behalf, all the effort I've made to find someone perfect for him who is also perfect for me, and it's come to this? No! I won't have it. I won't allow it! I'm speeding now past all the other cars on the highway, mind and rental car racing.

"Listen, Dad, I'm sure this is all just a misunderstanding. I know Florence likes you. Maybe we should go out to dinner tonight. I want to meet her anyway. Then if I decide she's wrong for you, you can break it off, okay?"

"So you'll be my second opinion?"

"Exactly. And make sure to reserve at a nice restaurant, okay?"

I arrive at his apartment just in time to get ready for dinner. Dad looks tired tonight, not his usual buoyant, boyish self, as he steps out of his bedroom in a nonstarter jacket and tie.

"Do you have any other pants, Dad?" I have to ask.

"Why? Are these dirty?"

"Olive green isn't good with a blue blazer. Khaki would be better."

"You're right," he says. "I don't know what I was thinking."

With a sigh, he returns to his closet and struggles into another pair of pants. I can see that even though his hip surgery is behind him, he's still in convalescence. It makes him look older than I'd like to see, a little more worn out than I'd expected.

"And do me a favor—at dinner tonight," I tell him as we're driving from his apartment building into the precious little city of Palm Beach, "don't make me recite all the things I've been doing for work lately. It makes me feel like I'm on display."

Typically he'd argue with me, even erupt in anger at my being too critical of him, then tell me to go back to New York. Tonight, he just nods in agreement.

"Whatever you say," he tells me.

He perks up when we get to the restaurant. It's a lively scene. Tabu, the in place for social snowbirds, is on Worth

Avenue, the town's window-shopping mecca. Every table
is full, and everyone looks intent on getting a good meal
for the money, their faces serious as they ask waiters
to turn down the air-conditioning or bring them more
bread. There's a pianist at a baby grand with a pinky ring
and toupee. He's attacking the keys with abandon. I'm
glad we got dressed up. It's a dressy kind of place, with
little tasseled lamps on each table throwing off pools of
flattering pink light that (along with the easily detect-
able plastic surgery in the room) erases years from every
face.

Florence is already at our table. She extends a hand
to say hello without getting up. Dad kisses her deferen-
tially on the cheek, then retreats to his seat, as if he's just
made a ceremonial bow before a queen. She's younger
than I thought, not more than halfway through sixty, I'd
guess. Not pretty exactly, put well put together. Auburn
hair gently coiffed, face and lips done just so. She's in
a charcoal cashmere twinset, with charcoal slacks to
match. Ralph Lauren, probably. Or maybe Michael Kors.
Very smart looking, far classier than anyone I'd imagine
for my father. While they make chitchat about the bridge
game she had just played that afternoon, I find myself
fantasizing about her various homes in Palm Beach, Sun
Valley, and Manhattan. Wouldn't it be nice to have holiday meals with her?

"How high is Sun Valley at?" Dad is asking.

"I'm not sure," she says. "High enough."

"Just wondering how the altitude is."

Oh, Dad, I'm thinking. I wish he wouldn't talk with his
mouth full of food. And he should have unbuttoned his
blazer when he sat down. He looks so stiff, sitting there,

like a child cowed at a grown-ups' table. He orders linguine. A mistake. He has no idea how to eat it properly. The way he's using that fork, it might as well be a tennis racket. I gesture for him to wipe the red sauce from his chin. He doesn't notice.

"Any plans for New Year's Eve, Bob?" she asks.

I change the topic. Politics. The 2004 election. We're into the second year in Iraq and things aren't going well at all. It's starting to fray Dad's nerves, tried-and-true Republican that he is. So while a war is raging abroad, he is fighting his own war down here with Democrats all around him, going at him like green flies in June. It wouldn't be so bad if he didn't feel he had to make it his mission to straighten everyone out about the reason for the war. But every time anyone at any dinner party or bridge table says anything disparaging about the administration, he rips into them. Florence, I can tell, is tired of it. He has embarrassed her more than a few times in front of her friends.

"Your father's quite opinionated about all kinds of complicated things," she tells me, as if he weren't sitting right here. "It can make for very heated conversations."

"I know you're thinking I don't know what I'm talking about, but I do," he says.

"You don't know what I'm thinking, Joe," she says. "You're not enough of a listener."

She's right about that. And I can't help admiring her for being well read, well dressed, and politically appropriate. For once my father is with someone plugged in and witty, and I'm feeling intoxicated with the refinement of her outfit. So instead of defending him, as a good son should, I gang up with her and shoot down everything he says.

And when he tries to get me to trade some of my lamb for his linguini by foisting his plate at me (something he does as a reflex at restaurants), I dismiss him.

"You know what I call trading each other's food like that?" I ask her.

"No, but your father does it all the time," she says, with a roll of her eyes.

"Jewish Ping-Pong," I say.

"Exactly! That's hilarious," she replies.

Then we both start cackling. And between the two of us, he looks like a little Mel Tormé voodoo doll in dress-up clothes, strapped to his chair. I don't think I've ever seen him looking so helpless. He quietly excuses himself and hobbles off to the men's room. He looks wobbly on his feet, like a toddler just learning to walk on his new hip, and I suddenly feel tender for him. He is a man, after all, who means no harm to anyone. She leans in and takes my hand with hers, which I can't help noticing is very cold and kind of like a claw. Her red nails (they match her lipstick) are like talons, her nose a little beak.

"Your father's a real piece of work," she says. "Isn't he?"

I down the rest of my merlot and nod. I suddenly feel hot inside. What gives her the right to call my father a piece of work? His quirkiness is his charm. Or part of it anyway. How dare she tease him about being her walker? How dare she toy with him, trot him around in front of her friends without having any feeling for him at all? And is there a man in all the Palm Beaches more eligible? I doubt it. He looks ten years younger than he is, and he's utterly self-sufficient and economically secure.

But I can see now that she is so not right for him. From

the hauteur of her hairdo down to the tasteful clasp on her Hermès bag and the bow on her Belgian loafer, it's clear this is no match. I don't know what I was thinking, pushing her on him. She makes him look so small, like a wriggling insect in her beak. It makes me grateful for the comfort he had with my mother, despite the tension, despite his urge to be away from the nest so much. Maybe she wasn't sophisticated, but she had grace and ease, and they had something lovely as a couple, even as he would rage, then apologize sweetly to her later. It was a good-enough marriage. Not easy, but worthy. And there was an acceptance between them that had to do with sharing a life together—kids, songs, the thrill of tulips and Passover macaroons. Best of all, Mom found his quirkiness funny and charming. Her laugh was a trill. Everything they did, even when she was unwell, had a Steve and Edie quality (sauntering across the suburban stage of life) that made them blend in harmony. This Florence, with all the wit and taste, has none of that.

When he comes back from the men's room (with the sauce wiped off his chin, thank goodness), he suggests we all go to a movie after dinner at the discount theater west of Lake Worth. There's a light comedy he wants to see.

"Isn't that a little lowbrow?" she asks.

"What would you recommend instead?" he asks.

"Well," she says as she gets up, "you'll have to forgive me. I'm a little tired. I'm going to call it a day. Thank you for a lovely dinner."

"Are you sure, Florence?" Dad says. "The night is young."

I want to nudge him under the table, tell him, Let her go, Dad. I was wrong. She's no good for you. You have to

want who wants you, who gets you, revels in you. But
who am I to give anyone advice about love? I stand up,
pull his chair out. He struggles to his feet, using the table
and me for balance.

"So then," she says, "good night."

Then she turns and leaves us there, with the bill to
pay.

A half hour later we are sitting in the living room of
his very white apartment in a very black mood. It's chilly
out. He wants the sliding doors closed. I want them open
but defer to his will. We're both a bit stunned, breathing
hard like two wildebeests that just escaped the claws of a
lioness. Bereft, alone, and feeling over the hill.

I've never felt so close to him, so wrapped up in his
life. And I've got my own love mess, too, making me spin.
Love is a minefield, a war. And we're two buddies in this
disaster movie. Or maybe it's a Comedy of Eros. How did
it come to this?

"My God, Dad. You were right! She's no good for you."

"That's what I was trying to tell you, Bobby."

"Why did you put up with her so long?"

"Because you told me to. I thought you might know
something I don't know about all this."

"Me? What the hell do I know about any of this? I know
nothing about love. I need a drink. You got anything?"

"Check the cabinet by the kitchen."

I race across his living room. I wish I could fix things
for both of us, but I feel so helpless. I open a mirrored
cabinet. You never know what you'll find in my father's
liquor cabinet. While growing up, I discovered all kinds
of bottles, as if it were a laboratory rather than a bar.
Bottles full of brightly colored liqueurs that only Jews

would have instead of hard booze. Lime green, sunny yellow. Sabra, which is a chocolate-and-orange Israeli liqueur in an "I Dream of Jeannie" bottle, consumed by Zionists and pre-diabetics. Adult parties in our home when I was a kid were never about drinking. They were about bridge. Sometimes charades. I have a photograph of my mother taken in the 1970s. She's in a psychedelic maxi skirt and purple blouse, on her knees, hands in the air, acting out a title of some book or movie. Her hair is unusually soft looking, the color just right. A Jewish Dinah Shore. Although she isn't young, she is exuberant and beautiful, the buoyant suburban sweetheart, laughing. She drank only the sweetest concoctions, crazy combinations for nondrinkers that my father mixed for her. Grand Marnier and ginger ale. Loganberry wine and apple juice.

"What's this?" I say as I pull out a bottle of calcified Irish Cream that leaves a sticky residue on my palm. "My God, how old is this?"

"I don't know, but it doesn't go bad," Dad says. "The alcohol acts as a preservative. I use it on my yogurt all the time."

"Ech!"

I wipe my hands on a cocktail napkin as if I've just touched battery acid. Then I pull out some Manischewitz, also unpleasantly sticky. There's something scrawled across the label of the half-empty bottle in his illegible handwriting.

"What's this, Dad? What's in here? I can't read this. What does it say?"

"Concord grape vodka."

"You're kidding, right?"

"It's a little experiment. Try some. And pour one for me while you're at it."

"Certainly!" I say. "Coming right up!"

I pull a couple glasses from his tiny lemon yellow kitchen and pour us drinks on the rocks. He sips his slowly. I slam mine down. Kosher cough syrup. I pour another.

He is sitting in his big chair by the TV. I sit on the couch next to him.

"Okay, I was wrong about Florence, totally wrong," I sigh.

"But I was glad to get a second opinion. I wasn't sure if it was me or her."

"So now what are you going to do? Anyone else on deck?"

"No. I'm a little at a loss right now, I'm sad to say."

"You usually have them lined up like fashion models on a runway."

"Lately every woman I meet seems to be trouble," he sighs. "And they all have something to complain about. Depressed children, ADD grandchildren, reflux, varicose veins, or some other unappealing thing."

"Not everyone can be happy living on the surface of things like you."

"I'm not asking for superficial," he sighs. "Just pleasant. But pleasant is in very short supply around here. Now Edie, she's a pleasant woman. I still have a thing for her, you know. But it's impossible. She's got both her other boyfriends down here right now from Philly, so I haven't heard from her in weeks."

"Dad, that woman is a seventy-five-year-old Jezebel."

"Seventy-five? Try eighty-six!"

Oh my God. I had no idea this woman jerking him around is that old. I pop up off the couch and lunge at his glass to get him a refill. I'd like to shake him to get some sense into him, get him to stop his pining. And while I'm at it, maybe I can get him to clean up this apartment. It's just such a mess.

"Eighty-six? Eighty-six? That's older than you, Dad! And the demographics are supposed to be in your favor! You're cute. You're fun. You should have your pick of the litter."

"Tell me about it," he says as he slurps his drink.

"Drink it down," I bark. "Don't be such a teetotaler. "

He chuckles and does as he is told, like a good son wanting to please.

"Have you ever met her other two boyfriends?"

"Yes, and they're both in their nineties. There should be no competition from what I can see. None! But she won't let them go. She isn't the kind of lady who wants to disappoint people. I guess it's not in her nature to reject anyone."

I kick off my shoes and flop back on the couch. "But it's in her nature to jerk you around?"

"Look, I can't explain it. I never thought I'd end up like this."

"I hear you, Dad," I say.

"Dating is a headache. There are just too many agendas and opinions. The other day I thought I was doing my friend Kal a favor setting him up on a double date with me and two ladies from downstairs for New Year's Eve."

"That's asking for trouble, no?"

"But you don't want to be caught short without a date for New Year's Eve around here, that's all I was thinking. It's the one time everyone needs a date."

"True," I say, as I lie back on his couch. The fortified Manischewitz is kicking in now. The rest of the world is falling away in this puddle of an alcoholic sugar stupor.

"So, to get things going, I arranged for us to have a pre-dinner, meet and greet the other morning, the four of us together for a nice brunch. Kal sees the woman I brought for him and decides right away she's too old. He wants someone twenty years younger. I was so irritated, I lost my temper. Now I've got nobody for New Year's Eve."

"I'm sorry to hear it."

"I am so close to giving up, Bobby, you have no idea."

Oh, yes, I do. But I don't say that. I'm not going to tell him about what I just went through with Ira. Yet in the buddy-movie version of what our lives have become here, I should be reaching out to him now, putting my arm around him, pulling him in tight like the son I'll never have, and telling him that, as messed up as it seems, he's on the right track because he's putting his heart out there, where it belongs. But how can I say anything like that when I'm so cynical about romance? I've given up on it. It's not worth the drama and humiliation.

"Okay, enough for now," I say. "I think we should just call it a night, pack it in, take a break from the love shredder. I'm going to bed."

I pull myself up, a little woozy. It's one in the morning.

"The cleaning lady changed the sheets for you," he says. "Towels are laid out."

"Okay. And Dad, would you mind closing your door tonight? The last time I was here, your snoring was louder than The Ring Cycle."

"Your mother never minded my snoring. "

"I know. She was a patient wife. I'm an impatient son."

"Who's going to want to put up with my snoring now?"

"I don't know, Dad. Just close your door tonight, okay? Good night."

When I get into the pullout bed in his guest room, it occurs to me that I snore, too. Would Ira put up with that? Would anybody ever want to put up with me? Outside, a lone cricket sings in the Florida night, or maybe it's a tree frog, calling out for a mate, desperate and shrill, repeating itself over and over. A freight train on the other side of Lake Worth whistles softly, a lovesick sigh.

There's a book by the guest bed, and I have to smile when I pick it up. It's a self-help bestseller about romance. Dad has been studying, I guess. I dislike self-help books, but I open it, and I page through. The author, a shrink who makes a lot of TV appearances, is bringing the act of falling in love down to earth. Hers is a bullying and authoritative tone: *Why aren't you happily married or partnered now? Older people are not good at dating because they are set in their ways. Head over heels isn't necessarily the best thing for love. Think about all the people you have dismissed! You never know what lurks within a person unless you give yourself time to find out.*

The message is clear, but my head is not from all the drinking.

Soon I'm asleep. In the middle of the night I sit up in bed and drink some water. Dad's door is open. He's not in his bed. On my way to the bathroom, I peer down the hallway into the living room and see him, watching TV. He's been an insomniac his whole life, a lonely affliction.

For a moment, I think about going in and sitting with him, staying up with him until he's ready for bed. But I'm too tired for that.

So, I lie in bed, thinking about him out there alone.

Are all children so haunted by their parents?

## CHAPTER 6

# And Bobby Makes Three

At nine o'clock the next morning, the phone wakes us up. I hear Dad fumbling for it in his bedroom. His "Hello" is groggy, then his tone changes to something muscular and energized, as if he suddenly gave himself a shot of testosterone.

"Well, hello, Edie!" he yells. "What a thrill to hear your voice!"

Her boyfriends number one and two are occupied for the morning, it turns out. So she has suddenly become free, and wouldn't it be nice to get together? Dad tells her yes without even bothering to ask how I feel about it. I'm at his bedroom door, and he is sitting in bed in his pajamas, so animated on the phone that he knocks down several pill bottles on his night table. After hanging up, he lumbers to his bathroom to run the electric razor on his already clean-shaven face.

"But, Dad, I was going to make you banana pancakes this morning."

"Let's do that tomorrow. It's a beautiful morning for a drive. And Edie asked that you join us. You'll like her, I guarantee it. You have a lot in common."

"Don't you understand you're never going to win her over, Dad?"

"I still have high hopes to make her mine. Maybe today will be the day."

I've never seen him hustling so fast. He shaves, splashes on aftershave, pulls out his best shirt—a bold check so natty that I wouldn't mind wearing it myself—the good penny loafers, and a festive sky blue sweater just back from the dry cleaner. Then he asks me how he looks. I tell him fine.

"But, Dad, I already went on a date with you last night. I can't be a third wheel again this morning. It's enough already. You don't need me for this."

"Don't think of Edie as a date. Think of her as a cousin. We'll go for a drive."

"I don't want to spend the morning in the car. I want to get some sun."

"So, let's take your convertible. You can be our chauffeur."

"You, Dad? In a convertible? I don't see it."

He doesn't like wind. He doesn't even like fresh air. This is a man as likely to get into the backseat of a convertible as go surfing, and yet, an hour later, I am in the parking lot of her building, watching him climb after her

into my backseat, new hip and all, like something between a Galápagos tortoise and a horny teenager.

"All aboard!" Dad crows.

I adjust my rearview mirror. Look at them back there.
She's in a Versace knock-off scarf and Jackie O sunglasses.
He has the sky blue V-neck tied around his neck—Mr.
Love Boat. "All set, you two?" I ask.

"Very cozy," he says. "Onward, driver!"

I pull out on Ocean Boulevard, a beautiful South Palm
Beach day. The sun is coming out from behind the clouds.
Birds are singing, traffic moving. The palms are sway-
ing, and there are flowers popping up everywhere, like
air kisses at a cocktail party. The wind is too loud for us
to have a conversation, and that's fine. What am I supposed to say to her anyway? I keep an eye on them in
my mirror. Dad's hair is blowing all over the place. I have
never seen him so happily wind-tossed. Any other day
he would not put up with all this weather, pleasant as it
might be. But today, he's young again, on a mission to
win her over. I can't help rooting for him.

As we pass Donald Trump's golf club, he's putting his
arm around her. Now he's resting his head against her
shoulder, and she's not pulling away. Geez. Should I even
be looking at this alter-kocker porn flick in my rearview
mirror?

I step on the gas and floor it across a bridge into West
Palm.

"Whee," she crows. "This is fun!"

"Bobby always shows me a good time," he says. "We're
a couple fun guys!"

I feel like something between a chaperone and drug
runner with these two kids in my backseat, high as kites.

On Flagler Drive, along the yacht-clogged waterway, he suggests we go to the Norton Museum.

"Pull in right there," he yells.

"That's not it," I yell back. But it is. I've missed the turn. Rather than explode the way he would when I dismiss his advice, he laughs and lets me pull around without further direction. What is the hormone she is emitting? I wish I could have it to sprinkle on him later, after she's gone. Inside the museum, which is full of friendly docents trying to make the most of their senior years by embracing the arts, I stroll alongside them as they hold hands like two kids going steady. She's got a nice little look. Her silver hair is cut short. The pink button-down and well-tailored slacks are flattering. She's trim and vital. I feel older than either of them right now, and exhausted, really. But then, this is the second time I'm the third wheel in two days.

How has my life come to this? I pick up a postcard in the gift shop of Edvard Munch's *The Scream*. Could anything express more precisely my state of mind?

Now we're back in the convertible, heading home.

The old man's having a ball with her back there. I turn on the radio.

They sing along and giggle into each other's faces. Then she leans back into him; they're cozy as kittens in the sun. Maybe he knows what he's doing. Maybe he's going to kiss her on the lips before we drop her off to get her to see he's the best thing that could happen to her and inspire her to leave behind boyfriends one and two. He's nuzzling her neck. It's not pretty. But in a way, it's just beautiful.

Might I learn something from him? His intention is so fierce, his craving for affection so pronounced. Love is everything, and he's unafraid to let her know it.

We're back on Ocean Boulevard now, the final stretch. With a last kiss and fierce declaration of love, is he going to make her see what a catch he is and turn her life around so that she will finally declare herself only for him and him alone? When we stop in front of her building, a white 1960s low-rise fantasia, he leans in and kisses her cheek, lets it linger there for longer than a moment. She pulls back, gives him a playful swat.

"Oh, Joe! You're the sweetest," she says. "This was fun, Bobby! Thank you so much for being our chauffeur! See you soon!"

Then she gets out of the car and walks away. Overhead, gulls call, laughing at us.

I am furious. But Dad doesn't look all that upset. In fact, he's all googly-eyed, as if he's just been touched by an AARP angel. He is smiling all the way home.

When we get to his apartment, he sits down, looking content. I pace his living room.

"What is she, out of her mind, with you and the two other boyfriends, Dad? Is this the three faces of Edie or something?"

"No," he laughs, sitting comfortably in his beige leather recliner, like something between a Bubba and a Buddha, "she's just a very nice woman who appreciates me."

"Yeah, a third of the time if you're lucky. *She* is nothing but a time-share, Dad. Why are you so stuck on her anyway?"

"Because she's easy to be with, just like your mother was. And she's foxy. We have chemistry."

I stop dead in my tracks. "Chemistry? At your age?"

And then he looks me in the eye and says, "Listen, with the pills they have today and the positive effects of the hernia surgery I had last year, I can go all night if I want to."

I'd like to run out the door. I resume pacing. "Okay, Dad. *That* is overshare. Enough. I think you're a fool settling for her."

He waves me off with a hand, as if he were hearing utter nonsense. "Bobby, please don't judge my happiness. If this is all I can get for now, I'll take it. Now what about you? How's your social life?"

"Thanks for asking. It's nowhere, as usual."

"So no prospects at all?"

I sit down. He wants me to share. I'll share. I kick off my sandals.

"Okay. I'll tell you. I met someone last month. He was terrific for a while."

"Good. And what was his name?"

"What's the difference? You think you know him? Ira, okay? His name's Ira."

He nods, mulls it over.

"Ira's a nice name. Can't go wrong with that. Tell me about him."

"He's great. Smart, funny, works in publishing."

"Sounds promising. What happened?"

"It just didn't work out."

"Why? Was it your fault or his?"

"I don't know. How would I know?"

I step out to the balcony. It really is a perfect sunny day for self-recrimination. My fault or his? Mine. I just wasn't sure he was the one. So I ran. I like things simple.

I like my space, my quiet. But I also hate my life. I step back inside and throw myself on the couch, while Dad sits in his chair. Now we have the full patient-therapist relationship—without any of the insight or training.

"Look, Dad, I tried, I failed."

"What happened?"

"I don't know. Maybe I was scared of disappointing him. I think he might want more than I know how to give. So we never even got started."

"Might. Maybe. Not very convincing, Bobby."

"My love life is a series of failures. I'm not cut out for being with anyone."

"That's not true. But you *do* like things the way you like them."

"Yes, and where do you think I got that from?"

He nods. "We're alike that way. But you really should be sharing your life with someone. You have so much to offer. You're a good person."

"Since when am I a good person?"

"You're a good person. Look how good you were to your mother."

"Me?"

"Look how good you've been to me this year, when I've been so lonely. You deserve happiness. Companionship. So why don't you try?"

"With who?"

"With this Ira. Stop running, stop thinking, stop questioning. Just try. And if it doesn't work out, maybe you should focus on something else I've been thinking about for you before you're too old."

"What's that?"

"I think you should consider becoming a father."

"What, Dad?"

"I said," he repeats evenly, "I think you should try to become a father."

"Oh really? And, um, how do you propose I do that?"

"Bobby, you have so many single lady friends who want to be mothers, and who I bet would just love to make a baby with you, however you do it."

"Never mind how we do it. The question is why," I'm shouting at him. "Why do you think it's so important that I have a child?"

He reaches over now, and takes my hand in his.

"Because," he says, "just look at what your mother and I got when we had you."

His words stun me, like when you come around the bend to a magnificent view of the sea or the mountains that you knew was there but never expected to see so suddenly.

I mean, wow. I could never say anything like that to anyone.

But maybe that's because I don't have anyone to say it to. I don't want to let this go. Alien as it is for me, I want to say something back, to let him know I heard him.

"That just might be the nicest thing anybody's ever told me, Dad," I finally say.

"Every word of it is true," he says.

## CHAPTER 7

# Auld Lang Resigned

When I get back to New York, I find myself doing something unheard of—taking my father's advice. I decide it wouldn't be a bad idea to e-mail an attractive lesbian couple I know who were recently joking with me about having a baby. Or should I say "gay-by"? Only how do I word it? *Sperm with your eggs?* I end up with something a little more straightforward.

*Hi Girls! Seasons Greetings! Hope this doesn't seem weird, but I want to let you know that if you ever do consider having a child, I'd love to help. Let's talk, ok? Bob*

Their reply appears in my inbox two days later. Is this the e-mail that will change my life forever, adding meaning and maturity, all without much responsibility? With some trepidation, I double-click for the answer.

*Bob! That's so sweet! But just so you know, yours is the fourth solicitation we've had this month from a gay male friend. What's with you people? Anyway, we're flattered and thank you for thinking of us in that way. We'll keep you on file. Happy New Year!*

What happy New Year? My mother is gone. My father is insane. My brother and his wife and kids are away at some expensive Caribbean resort. And I'm alone in their apartment on the oh-so-parental Upper West Side (sippy cups! double-wide strollers!) without a date for New Year's. There are two cats and one guinea pig to look after. The cats pretty much avoid me. They can see I'm in a bad mood. I look out at all those other apartment windows out there, full of couples and families, fanning out from here into New Jersey and on to Pennsylvania and then eternity. All those lives. Sometimes I see couples arguing in kitchens or rushing in foyers, getting ready to go out. I tell myself that life is unpleasantly noisy and complicated in all those apartments, in all those families and relationships. Those lives—listening to each other, worrying about each other—are just so full of conflict and compromise. I tell myself I'm lucky I'm free. But to do what?

Most friends are out of town. I don't feel like seeing the ones who are around. I file a column about the conundrum of how to break off boring friendships. I order in and read the daily papers. I think about calling Ira, but don't. How is it possible to have this privileged life and be so miserable?

One night I get a call from Dad. I haven't heard from him since I got back from Florida. Now I know why. He's met someone. Or perhaps I should say re-met someone. The first time they were introduced at the home of friends across the road, he didn't given her much thought. After one date, he wasn't feeling anything. A few weeks later, in the aftermath of Florence and Edie, he found the strength to give this woman another try. Suddenly, things are happening between them, all kinds of things. So many things, I feel like I'm listening to a kid at camp describing a really good week.

"Her name is Doreen," he says. "She's a very cultured lady, well read, sociable, and very active. Also Jewish-minded, but not overbearing about it."

They are going out together every night, he's telling me, to concerts, movies, lectures, and dinners with each other's friends. Better yet, she has been cooking for him, something he loves, not just because it saves him the expense of paying for their dinners, but because it gives him comfort to be eating homemade meals at a kitchen table.

"Her cooking is almost as good as Mom's," he says.

My mother's cooking was anything but good. She was certainly not the gourmet my brother would have liked. That would entail spending money on fine ingredients and taking a more sophisticated approach to cuisine than is possible in a kosher, microwave-driven home. And like so many housewives of her time, she had the added onus of trying to cut back on both our sugar and cholesterol. My brother and I ended up snickering at recipes made with artificial ingredients of unknown provenance. Generic instead of name brands. Cyclamates instead of sugar. Diet margarine instead of butter. Artificially flavored gelatin and tubs of nondairy whipped cream that might have been better suited for waxing the station

wagon. "Love Canal pie," we dubbed one such dessert.
Mom just laughed. "You two are such critics," she said.
We never gave much thought to how hard she worked on
what she prepared. But my father loved everything she
served him, which is not to say he didn't doctor things
once she placed them on the table. He poured salad dressing on her lasagna, applesauce on her casseroles, and had
a handy bottle of artificial raspberry syrup for many of
her well-meaning confections. I can still see him sitting
at our round kitchen table, puppy-dog-happy with all
there was to eat in his bowl.

"Step on his foot and he opens his mouth," my mother
used to cluck.

And now, he has finally found someone to feed him
the same way. A Doreen. And I can tell it's serious. There
is none of the tentative quality in his voice he's had with
so many other women he's fished up and tossed back this
year. She cooks for him. He sings to her. They dance in
the elevator. They are excited about New Year's Eve tomorrow night, with plans to attend a synagogue dinner
dance. This could finally be the one. But I want to know
what we're getting into here.

"I have a few questions," I say.

"Of course," he replies. "Be my guest. I'll be happy to
tell you what I know."

I sit down on the window ledge, looking out over Manhattan as it falls into winter dusk. I'm holding a pencil
and tapping it on a pad, as if I were a reporter on a crime
case.

"Where does she live?"

"Her building is called the Seacrest. It's south of the
Lake Worth Bridge."

"South? That's not as nice as where you are. Is it a good building?"

"Very nice, on the ocean side. And she has a huge apartment."

"Really? Ocean view?"

"No. Ground floor, a three-bedroom."

"Ground floor? Oh. And where does she live in the summer?"

"She stays in Florida."

"Really? She must not be so well off then, huh? And is she attractive?"

"Fair, not bad. She wears a wig, I think."

"A wig? What is that, Orthodox?"

"No, she has some minor condition, not serious."

"Well, I don't know about you, but I'm not sold, Dad."

"Why? She's a lovely person with a good figure. And we're having a ball. I don't think I've been this thrilled with a woman since your mother was well."

"Oh, *really* now!"

"I wish you wouldn't be so cynical."

"Me? Cynical?"

"Doreen isn't perfect, but she's perfect for me. Listen, it's a decision to see how wonderful someone is, flaws and all. That's what it takes to find a match. Love is a decision, Bobby. But what about you? Do you have a date for tomorrow night?"

"I don't need one. I'm staying in."

"Did you call this Ira fellow, like I suggested?"

"No. But you'll be pleased to know that I did e-mail some lesbians about making a baby."

"You did? Good for you!"

Such delight in his voice. He's not used to hearing that I've taken his advice.

"But they turned me down."

"Too bad. At least you asked, you tried. Now what about this Ira?"

"I'm sure he's moved on from me by now."

"You don't know that. But you have to let your guard down. Call him, see if he has a New Year's date. And don't be so quick to judge this time. Give him a chance. You have to stop looking for perfection, Bobby. That's the only way you'll find it."

"What is this, Dad? Tuesdays with Morris?"

He laughs. I can see his smile as if he's in the room, as dopey as it is dazzling.

"Listen, I have to get off now," he says. "I've got an errand."

"Where you off to, lover boy?"

"I have to go pick up my white dinner jacket. I'm renting it for tomorrow night."

"Dad! Isn't a white dinner jacket for summer?"

"I don't know, and I don't care. I love white dinner jackets. So does Doreen. We'll take a picture so you can see how nice it looks. But listen, I'm going to make her late if I don't get off the phone. Happy New Year! Over and out!"

He hangs up on me. And I sit there listening to the dial tone. I'm a little thrown. I'm always the one rushing the old man off the phone. He just hung up on me? Yes, because he has too much to do to chew my ear off tonight. Twenty floors below, the traffic signals go from red to green all the way down Broadway. *Stop looking for perfection, that's the only way you'll find it.* Did he just cough up the hairball of meaning I've been looking for from him my whole life? I place the phone back on the wall. His words resonate in my ears. I once heard that when you know how to listen, everyone's the guru. Could Joe Morris actually be so wise? Am I single because I don't know how to love who loves me? And is it actually possible that you really are nobody until somebody loves you?

CHAPTER 8

# Auld Lang Realigned

pace around the apartment all evening. I can feel something pushing me, as if I'm guided by Dad's voice, possessed. He may not be so worldly. But he's been so brave about love. Why have I spent so much of my adult life afraid of it? I take a deep breath, then march to the phone and call Ira. "Hey, what's up?" he says, just like that. Our conversation flows easily. It isn't hard to ask what he's doing for New Year's Eve.

"What are *you* doing?" he responds. Effortless. Direct. He doesn't need to be coy or play games. Despite the fact that he's younger, better looking, and more accomplished than I am, he's still interested in me. And he doesn't feel he has to hide it.

We decide I'll make dinner, then we'll go out to some parties.

The following night I open the door in my black velvet jacket to find him with flowers, champagne, and appetizers, rosy-cheeked from the cold. He steps inside and takes off his topcoat to reveal a burgundy sharkskin suit. His loafers are Gucci, patent leather. It's an outfit that dares to outshine mine, and a little loud for winter, I can't help thinking. In less than a minute, he is all over my kitchen, running around doing this and that, with a happy and officious abandon. "How are you preparing that lamb?" he barks. "Don't overcook it! That's the worst thing you can do!" He nudges me aside to get to my oven and sticks his nose in it. Then he goes off to lay out the gravlax and crackers he brought from Dean & Deluca. I would never shop at such an expensive food store, not for myself or anyone else. But along with his fixation on quality clothing, hair products, and linens, he is obsessive about food. It has to be of the highest quality, the freshest, the leanest, the most expensive. When he brings me a slice of his gravlax, impeccably garnished with capers and a dollop of crème fraîche on pumpernickel, I swoon.

I take the lamb out of the oven and start carving it. Ira hovers. I'm anxious. I don't need anyone in the kitchen, looking over my shoulder like a culinary conscience, judging what a lazy, clueless chef I am. "Hey! That's not how you slice a lamb," he says. "Give me that carving knife and get out of my way!" I laugh a nervous laugh and step aside. Who is this person in my kitchen? A pushy personality with a loud voice, loud suit, hair and nose almost as large as my own, and shtick so shticky I call him Shecky.

"What do Michael Jackson and Kmart have in common?" he asks, as I pop the champagne he brought. "Boys' pants—half off!"

"Oy" is all I can manage in reply.

Later, he is very attentive to my three dinner guests, old college pals whom I don't see often. We made last-minute plans to get together, and I worried they wouldn't connect with Ira. But everything flows wonderfully. He's a great conversationalist. Well, who wouldn't be amused to hear him talk about becoming a donor dad? It turns out a couple of his good lesbian friends sought him out for the job. So Ira went through the proper medical tests, signed some papers giving up paternity to keep things simple, and then, one night not long ago, with a full moon shining, he got their call to come by, and delivered his goods in a baby-food jar that he had boiled to be sterile.

"And now my friend is three months pregnant," he says. "I hit it on the first try."

My guests laugh. And I find myself beaming at the possibility of a little child in our lives. The idea of becoming some kind of a new uncle with Ira is delicious. I know I'm ahead of myself. But it's New Year's Eve, the first one that I'm not alone for in years.

In the kitchen, he moves so expertly that serving dinner is effortless. I feel relaxed in a way that I never am when I entertain. He's so capable, energetic, and amusing—my friends are charmed. So am I. I sit back and, without having to do a thing, watch everyone enjoying one another in a way that strangers rarely do on New Year's Eve. It's as if we've been entertaining as a couple forever.

Later, we drop by to see his friends around the corner.

Then we hit a posh New Year's Eve party at Trump Tower. It's a raucous crowd of wannabes and already-ares, guests in their thirties and forties. Dapper men, thin women with plump lips. Actor here. Author there. It girls. Implants. Veuve. And every bartender looks like an underwear model, lifting bottles at the bar like barbells. The apartment is TV-money glamorous, with views of Central Park and a high ceiling smothered in black balloons that resemble giant mounds of caviar. I'm pleased with myself for taking Ira to a hot New Year's party. And he's smart enough to know how to enjoy it.

When he talks to people, his hybrid Bronx/London lockjaw puts me on edge. But everyone he meets seems delighted. As I watch him talk to a journalist he knows, I feel proud to be with him. So what if he's wearing a shiny suit? Who cares if he looks more like me than any man I ever imagined I could be with? We complement each other well.

"Are you two brothers?" one drunk blonde asks while we're getting our coats.

"Of a sort," Ira says.

"What an obnoxious question," I say after we've left the party and are walking up Central Park West. "Why would you even answer her?" I weave along the sidewalk, high on too much champagne. The branches above us are shining, coated in ice. The trees outside Tavern on the Green are coated with tiny blue and white lights. Out of some window high above us, I hear noisemakers and singing, corks popping.

"I hate that," I say. "I hate that someone would think we look alike."

"We don't look alike. We're both Semitic, that's all, with salt-and-pepper hair."

"Do people actually think I'm dating you because you

look like me? I don't want to go out with myself! Do they actually think I could be that much of a narcissist?"

"Don't take this the wrong way, but aren't you?" he says. "Anyway, what do you care what some drunk woman at a party thinks of us?" He shakes his head. He smiles, then bursts out laughing, which makes me laugh.

"What's so funny?" I ask.

"You, Bob Morris, are the most untherapized Jew I have ever met."

He's right about that. He sounds so knowing, this prince from the kingdom of the Bronx, spawning ground of Calvin Klein and Ralph Lauren. There is something both dignified and funny about Ira. Something a little Seinfeld and a little Leonard Bernstein, both men of Central Park West, where we're walking right now. The fact that I have to stop to relieve myself behind a tree next to the Museum of Natural History doesn't fluster him. He just shakes his head and slows his walk so I can catch up when I'm through. At the corner of West Eighty-first Street, couples in black tie hail cabs. Others step out of buildings, with high heels clicking against frozen sidewalks. I have never loved New Year's Eve like I am loving it tonight. We pass a grand old entrance to a towering doorman building that Ira stops to admire.

"You know what? This is the building of my first therapist," he says. "I was fifteen when I came here."

"Fifteen? That's young for therapy."

"When my mother found out I was gay, she thought I should go. I chose this particular psychotherapist because I liked her building. She was a Jew with skis and tennis rackets in the closet, and I found that attractive."

"You're worse than I am," I say.

"But I'm not self-hating like you are," he replies.

Later I'll find out about his various addictions and rehabs through his twenties—a night in jail for trying to buy cocaine, interventions when he was taking heroin—that sort of thing. For now, I feel titillated by how much more there is to know about this man who's younger than me by several years. We are alone as we walk west on Eighty-sixth Street. But I feel a lot of eyes upon us now. There are the eyes of all my friends, who have seen how carelessly and cluelessly I have treated love in the past. There are the eyes of my ex-boyfriends, every one fair-haired and attractive to me, but none nearly as capable as Ira of making me feel comfortable. I wonder if my mother is watching us tonight, too, from up above. And what about my father? He must be home by now, after his white-dinner-jacket night with Doreen. Are they sleeping together? Banish the thought. But bless the man. It is his eyes more than anyone's I feel on me right here and now, in the first hours of this New Year. He insists I'm capable of loving. I stop and throw my arms around Ira.

"Happy New Year," I say. "I'm going to become a better person on your back!"

"On my back?"

"On your clock, on your dime!" I'm staggering on the sidewalk. "I'm going to learn to be a better boyfriend and a better person!"

"You're obnoxious when you're drunk," he says. "But kind of sweet."

Then he leans in and nuzzles me with his big nose.

It ends in a kiss. Our noses negotiate like horses in a field, snout to snout.

A few flakes of snow drift down from the sky as we reach home.

I wake up the next morning to a sky of slate gray clouds and a bright feeling in my soul. Ira breathes softly beside me. He looks so innocent asleep. His skin is rosy. I am hungover. Which means I was snoring last night. But I guess he didn't mind. I guess he slept right through it. Many in the past have complained about my snoring. Maybe we really are meant to be together.

I can't wait for him to wake up so we can start the day.

This man who isn't who I thought I wanted is exactly what I needed.

And so it begins for real. All of it, the full, unchecked heart-on-your-sleeve, foot-in-your-mouth experience of real love. He harangues and I hock. He hisses and I spit. Then we laugh and make up and keep going.

He hates that I leave cabinet doors open and make a mess when I cook.

"That's not the way to make a bed," he barks.

"Why are you so compulsive? And how do you know anyway?" I ask.

"I learned it in rehab. We had to make our beds army style."

He doesn't like it if we can't sleep together every night, even though our relationship is still very young, and I want to keep things on a medium burn.

"You're an addictive personality," I complain.

Well, what he loves he loves. At night he wants to sleep entwined. For a while, it makes me laugh, how he scrambles around under the sheets to be in my arms. I can't sleep. "You have to give me a little space," I say.

"You'll learn to share," he says.

Will I? I start polling couples to see if they sleep entwined. One day I ask my friend Amanda, an easygoing young wife, and she tells us there's no way she can fall asleep with her husband wrapped around her. "It just doesn't work for me," she says.

"See?" I tell Ira. "I'm not afraid of intimacy. I'm just a normal sleeper!"

He doesn't argue. But he also doesn't give me more space. He's aggressively affectionate. He needs me to turn over so he can hold me this way or that way. Sometimes he needs his back rubbed. His feet rubbed. I have to fight all my selfish urges to accommodate him. And to my surprise, it feels good to try. But it also makes me incredibly anxious. Are we in this too deep?

Who is this man, and how did we settle in so fast?

I worry about his health. He has to take Nexium every day. And what's with all the sleeping pills? Is he healthy enough for me to take on? It's been a year and a half since my mother died, but I'm still not as sure as I'd like to be about the in-sickness-and-in-health aspect of commitment. I want the healthiest possible specimen.

The real problem with Ira is that he is such a big presence. He calls on the phone all day when I need quiet to focus on work. He questions every one of my emotional blunders. He makes me tell him why I love him when he knows I never talk like that.

"Maybe you're just incapable of being in a couple," he says.

"Maybe you're incapable of ever being alone," I reply.

I think of my parents, and the conflicts they had in their good-enough marriage. Was it worth giving up all

those parts of themselves to have a life together? Then
I think of all my own failed attempts at relationships,
all the men who'd take forever to even use the word *boyfriend* to describe me, and then we would only want to
be together once or twice a week, so we could have our
space. Is there even such a thing as being cautiously in
love? With Ira it is immediate and total. I am never alone
now; even when he's at the office, there are e-mails and
calls to me at my desk at home. What I've got on my
hands is a pushy, high-strung, needy, knowing, amusing,
and terribly generous man who is making my life—even
with Dad out of my hair now with his new love—into a
big, sweet, sticky, out-of-control thing that scares me to
death.

It's Valentine's Day weekend, our first trip together.
Bal Harbour, Miami. City of old Jews, reflux, and retail.
Our hotel room is chic and modern, but very small for
two big personalities. Ira scurries around unpacking
every single piece of luggage, laying out all the bottles of
pills and all his overpriced hair and skin products on the
bathroom counter. I would prefer someone more rugged,
into nature, not Neutrogena. He's being kind of fussy,
slamming drawers and complaining about the quality of
the linens and towels. It makes me more anxious than I
already am, and I start wondering if the traffic noise on
Collins Avenue is going to keep me awake tonight after
he finally calms down. Then I wonder if the combination of a small hotel room and four days with nothing
to do but find fault will make me revert back to being
the naturally impossible person I don't want to be in a
couple. I'm desperate to relax. Stepping out onto the balcony and looking out at the ocean, I think about want-

ing to embrace all of Ira, not just the parts I like. I want
to be more accepting and less critical of this man who's
a better partner than I deserve. But how do I love his
loud voice, wiry hair, and irritability? He can be so high-
strung and sensitive, and that can be hard for someone
like me, who is used to spouting off callous things without much thought. He doesn't miss a goddamn trick. And
it drives him crazy when I don't shut every single closet
and cabinet drawer.

He smokes too much. He plans too much. He needs
too much.

Inside, he lights up a cigarette and throws himself onto
his laptop. It's the weekend, I'm thinking, what could be
so important? But he's pounding away at that thing so
compulsively. Then he makes business calls to L.A. and
starts tearing apart the room looking for a manuscript
he misplaced. Soon there are pages all over the bed. One
minute he's complaining about slow Internet access. The
next about the shampoo the hotel has provided. He is all
histrionics and hysteria. I step outside again, close the
balcony door, and try to read. But he comes out and sits
on my lap and wants to kiss. I gently push him away. He
resists, then tries to nuzzle my ear. "Stop! I'm reading," I
tell him. He takes offense at that, so we have to spend the
next ten minutes talking about it.

"Why don't you like to be touched?" he asks.

"Why don't you have any boundaries?" I reply.

God! How do people do this?

Later we're walking along the beach under a cloudy,
neon-lit sky. It's not exactly pristine, but it's kind of romantic just the same. Clouds are glowing pink. Seabirds
are drifting shadows overhead. There isn't a soul on the

sand. All kinds of things are going through my head. Will this relationship survive? And what in the world will I do if it doesn't? But we walk in silence, our bare feet sloshing in the foam. He looks adorable in his old jeans and Nantucket sweatshirt. I have no idea why I'd have any doubts about such a catch. He lights a cigarette and coughs a little, a smoker's cough. It scares me, and I realize that even though we've been together only a couple of months, I'd be completely lost without him. Then I do something I never do. I take his hand. We walk in silence. I have my ukulele in my backpack—thought it might be nice to serenade him. But he's such a sophisticated man, so flip and sarcastic, that I have to wonder if he's going to laugh at my singing. We climb up on a lifeguard chair. He lights another cigarette. I chug my beer, all nerves. What did my father say? Love is a decision?

I take my ukulele out of my backpack.

"What the hell is that?" he asks.

"Shh," I whisper. Then I strum and sing.

*There were bells on the hill*
*But I never heard them ringing,*
*No I never heard them at all*
*Till there was you.*

I sing very tentatively with my head down. But then the moon comes out from behind the clouds, turning the whole world opalescent white. And I raise my head and look out to sea, and throw myself into the little love song with everything I've got.

*And there was music,*
*And there were wonderful roses,*
*They tell me,*
*In sweet fragrant meadows of dawn,*
*And dew.*

*There was love all around,*
*But I never heard it singing,*
*No I never heard it at all*
*Till there was you.*

When I finish, I take a swig of beer and look at Ira, and there are tears in his eyes.

"Wow," he says more softly than he's ever spoken to me before. "I never expected that from you. Where did it come from?"

I don't say anything. But I know when he meets my dad, who taught me everything I know about singing from the heart, he'll figure it out.

PART IV

# Love's Labors Won

## CHAPTER 1

# Inspecting Doreen

There is nothing like a blossoming tree in Manhattan. Who expects such bright clumps of white, yellow, and pink in this dark dirty town? But there they are, outside my window, turning the city into something like a junior prom or maybe a valentine to itself. It's late May now, and I'm feeling anxious, getting dressed to meet Doreen, the new woman in Dad's life. He's back in Great Neck from Palm Beach for the summer. I've been keeping up with his new life by phone. Since he's been back up north, he's been running around like a happy little goat in a field of fresh grass and rubbish. There were times over the winter when I was keenly aware that he was calling me from her apartment, maybe even her bedroom. It took a little getting used to. Now she's come up from Florida for an extended visit and is having a ball with him, the happy host. Last night they stayed in a Marriott in lower Manhattan. He had a half-price coupon. So the lovebirds are trysting in the big city for a moment. It has been six months for them now, as it has been for Ira and me. After his year of dating dangerously, Dad's firmly in love.

"It's a full-blown romance," he says. "You'll like her, I know it."

So on a warm and sunny afternoon, I'm leaving my tidy apartment, where Ira has made the bed impeccably, as he does every morning before leaving for his office. Then I cross the West Side Highway and start walking down to meet Dad and Doreen at an outdoor restaurant near Battery Park. The pedestrian path along the Hudson River is full of adorable people, shirtless guys, women in sports bras, couples holding hands as they glide along on Rollerblades, enjoying New York Harbor. I don't feel my usual resentment today, not even toward the cutest couples. Why should I when I've got love myself? But that doesn't mean I don't feel anxious. I'm meeting the woman my father plans to be with for the rest of his life. What will she look like? Sound like? It's an odd situation to have to welcome a whole new personality into our small family. As I walk, my heart pounds hard, like the waves against the moorings. I don't see him in the lunchtime crowd at the restaurant. Then all at once I do. Yes, there he is. There they are, the happy couple. There should be a pink neon heart over their heads.

"Hello, Robert!" my father says. "What a thrill you could join us!"

Doreen is a slim woman in a cream silk blouse and navy slacks. She's blond, or, I should say, her wig is. She smiles an unstrained, easy smile as she gets up and opens her arms to embrace me. Should I kiss her or just shake her hand? I panic and stand frozen, hands at my side. But she pulls me in for a warm embrace and a "Mwuh" on the cheek.

"It is such a thrill to meet you," she says. "You are all your father talks about!"

She isn't drop-dead gorgeous. But her skin is smooth and peachy, her dark eyes bright. And for mid-seventies, she looks great. Her clothes aren't fancy, but they're tasteful. The only thing that bothers me is her wig. It could be nicer. But then, so could I. Why am I even thinking about it?

"When I was growing up, this park didn't even exist," she's saying. "Now it's a whole world down here."

The voice is one of a city woman, but not a society lady. Educated but not overly refined. Without much prompting, I'm getting her full story, with Dad filling in as she goes. Her early years were spent as a journalist. She's writing a book on Soviet Jews.

"You two have a lot to talk about," Dad says, mouth full of focaccia.

I do want to like her. They get along so well. They play Jewish Ping-Pong with their food and share with hardly a negotiation. They order a cheesecake and eat from the same plate like kids over a malted milk shake. Then she asks the waiter for a refill on her cappuccino.

Right away, I know that's not allowed, and I blush.

"I'll have to charge you," he says.

"Oh, come on," she replies. "Let me see the manager."

It's just a little thing. But it makes me uncomfortable. My mother, parsimonious as she was, would never push like that. I excuse myself and go to the men's room to call my brother at his office. He's not in. Ira isn't available either. I'm anxious to talk to someone, vent my silly anxieties, purge myself of my nonsense so I can go back out there and sit back down in a more open-minded and welcoming way. Then, as I walk back to the table, I notice how right they look together. She is laughing as she feeds him cheesecake as if on a honeymoon. And under the table, he's holding her hand. I feel my emotional claws retracting as I sit back down.

"You know what I loved?" she says to me. "When you described your father in one of your columns as a well-meaning iconoclast. That captures him so well."

"He isn't the world's easiest guy," I say. "Have you noticed?"

"Sure, but he's full of fun, and we're having a wonderful time together. He's put a shine on my life that I never thought would be possible at my age."

"How long did it take for you to click?" I ask.

"On our third date I had him over for dinner, and I just knew," she says.

"She made tilapia, and it was marvelous," Dad adds.

"Remember the night you turned up the music and danced with me on your balcony," she says, as she straightens his hair. "You really swept me off my feet, Joe."

"You are entirely sweep-able," he says.

She chuckles, leans in against him, and says, "What about when you came over with flowers from the Winn-Dixie and sang that parody you wrote? I was stunned."

"I have a copy of it right here," he says. I hope he's kidding. But he reaches into his wallet and pulls out a paper with typed lyrics and, without taking a breath, sings.

*I bought some nice flowers for a sweet lady*
*Mr. Dixie had the Winn-ing ones.*

"This is so cute," she says as he goes on. "I was so flattered."

*I hope that my selection bought her some fun*
*She has earned the title of my honey bun . . .*

This isn't our backyard or balcony, where we sing in
private. We're in public here, in my sophisticated city,
and so, even at my age, I can't help feeling like an adolescent, embarrassed by my uncontrollable father. But he
just keeps singing, and she is nodding along, her head
bobbing happily, and it's impossible not to be warmed by
the whole thing, even as my face blushes red as Chianti.

*Wrapped up some nice petals that I hope will thank her*
*For her many kindnesses to me . . .*
*Sure hope she likes this tune,*
*'Cause I'm coming over soon*
*For some kisses and a great big spoon!*

It's utterly cornball, of course. But I have to say, there
is something so lovely about how she is charmed by him,
the same way my mother had been charmed by him. And
I can see, as clear as her nail polish, that this Doreen,
wig and all, is nothing less than the perfect match for the
old man. No, she isn't quite as impeccable as I require.
But she has this way of looking us both in the eye and
listening just the way my mother did. And really, after
watching him date all year, it's obvious to me that some-

one as nice as my mother is all we really need again in our family.

Lunch finished, my father pays the bill, and we get up to go.

"How about we walk a little?" I ask as we leave the restaurant.

"Oh yes, it would be nice to look at the river," she says.

"You two go ahead," my father says. "I'll wait right here."

Some things will never change. Even in love, he's lazy and obstinate. And even today I cannot stop myself from trying to inspire him to do things he doesn't want to do.

"Come on, Dad, join us," I say. "Walking is good for your circulation. You have to keep your heart in shape. You know that. Use it or lose it!"

He finds the nearest bench and plops himself down.

"Dad! Come on! Just a few steps! You can see the Statue of Liberty!"

"Please, Bobby, just let me be. Go, enjoy."

"For God's sake, Dad, we're asking you to join us!" For a moment I'm thrown back to every fight we've ever had.

Doreen just smiles and shakes her head. She seems to understand what I'm going through. "It's okay, you go ahead, Bobby," she says, as she turns to sit with him. "We know you're busy. Go back to your life. Don't worry about us. We'll sit here and enjoy the view and argue about politics. Maybe we'll see you later."

I don't know what to say. I'm not needed, so I'm free to go. It's a strange feeling, perhaps, the closest I'll come to seeing a child of my own settling into love for the first time. I stand looking at them another moment—lovers in the sunshine by the river.

Then I say good-bye, turn, and walk away without feeling guilty, leaving him with her on that bench and knowing he's in very loving hands.

We both are now.

## CHAPTER 2

# Nice to Meet You

Right after that, I realize I'm ready for Dad and Ira to meet. It's time. After six months, we are definitely a couple. We've been at his place or mine every night. We're talking about moving in together, getting a domestic partnership contract from City Hall, which is about as married as gays can be in New York, even if, as one friend described it, it's more like getting a parking permit than a marriage license. We go out together to all kinds of dinner parties, careful not to dress too similarly so that we don't get asked if we're brothers. He is as paternal as he is romantic, incredibly helpful with my career, and I feel both protected and the need to protect him at every turn. And all the lip service I've paid to the power of being single has disappeared into the pollen-laden air of late spring. We've been to Paris together, where I had the hubris to think I could make him quit smoking. We've been to Bermuda, where we got into a fight after I made fun of his obsession with face cream, then threw my back out because I felt so bad. Before leaving the island, we took a picture of us together on the beach where my parents honeymooned in 1951.

He is a man who knows what he wants as much as or more than I do. So every few weeks, we fight, and he says it's over between us, and walks out the door or storms away from me on the street, then comes back two minutes later to apologize. It has taken a while to realize that all this conflict is healthy, part of the investment in something that could be for the rest of our lives. It's strange to feel so optimistic. Maybe in middle age, romance is a more sustainable commodity than when you're young.

"I got the oldest puppy in the pound," Ira says about me.

There isn't a day when I don't look at him and find him beautiful.

So he's met and charmed my brother and his family and regaled them with tales of how impossible I am. And I have met his three siblings and his little white-haired mother, a fireplug of a Bronx woman who is as liberal as an eighty-two-year-old woman can be.

And now it's time for Ira to meet Dad, who volunteers to drive into the city to take us to dinner. He's taking us to a nice place. His idea, not mine, which both pleases me and throws me for a loop. I open my door one May evening, and I can't believe it. He is in the most impeccable sports jacket. Black-and-white check, with a subtle trace of electric blue. Classy. Beyond my wildest dreams.

"My God, Dad! Where did you get that?"

"Brooks Brothers. I thought you'd like it."

"Were they having a sale?"

"No. I saw it in the window and liked it so much I went inside to try it on. It slipped on like silk. I never felt such soft wool, like something *you* would wear. So I asked the price. Five hundred dollars! For a sports jacket, no trousers even! But then I thought, *Well, what the heck? I like it!* And I thought about how much you'd like it, too."

This is as unlikely a scenario as I've ever heard him describe. Yet, here he is, standing before me, telling me he paid full price for something well made and stylish.

"Wow, Dad" is all I can say as I mix him a ginger ale with orange juice.

"I kept thinking I'd return it," he says, "but I wanted something nice for tonight."

He models it for me, turning around. He could be my son, looking for my approval. And he can have it. He looks so smooth, so young, as if he'll live forever. But I do wonder if he could have done better with his tie.

"Dad, you look like a million bucks. But are you sure about that tie?"

"I love this tie. But what's the trouble? Not the right colors?"

That and so many other things about it are wrong.

"Your jacket's checked and your tie is striped, and also, what is this fabric?" I ask, as I slide my finger over something synthetic and washable. "Acetate?"

"So I don't have to worry about spilling," he says, slurping his drink.

"I think I have just the thing, Dad. Hang on."

I leap to my closet and pull out my favorite tie—Gucci, solid electric blue. We're running late, but he doesn't argue about trying it on. He steps into my bathroom and, with slightly trembling hands, removes his tie and puts on mine. I've never stood with him at a mirror before, but I am reminded now how alike we are. Our eye color is exactly the same shade of hazel. He finishes tying the tie and then steps back to admire himself.

"Very nice," he tells me. "This is just perfect. Thank you."

He looks handsome. I am so proud. And as I straighten my tie on him, face-to-face, close as we've ever been, I imagine it going for a dip in his soup bowl at dinner, or perhaps having a gentle encounter with his butter knife. But that's okay. Even if my favorite tie doesn't survive, I think there's a pretty good chance that we will now. I can't wait for Ira to see him looking so dapper. And yes, I know style shouldn't mean so much to me. It shouldn't be about the cut of his trousers or the color of a tie. It shouldn't be about the sports jacket, either, but the man who is inside it. But, wait: actually, what *is* inside his sports jacket? As we head for the door I'm noticing that there's a pronounced little *lump* down there in his pocket, ruining the line.

"Dad, is there something in that pocket?"

He pats it gently, then has a realization.

"Oh, *that's* where it is," he says, as he pulls out a ball of tissue with a slight speckling of blood. "I've been looking all over for this."

"What is it?"

"I lost a piece of my tooth last month on a toasted bagel. Now I can bring this into my dentist to see if he can use it instead of a crown. Ready for dinner?"

"If you put that tooth away, I might be."

So we go to dinner, where we meet up with Ira. And of

course he and my father get on as if they've known each
other their entire lives. Dad's manners are typically his
own. And Ira's are impeccable. But somehow it doesn't
matter. Their voices are of equal volume, and their lack of
inhibition strangely similar. I find myself at times wanting to intercede and correct them. But they're off and
running, comfortable as old friends, and don't need me
controlling the conversation. They tell each other shticky
jokes. They compare notes on the Ambien and Nexium
they take. Ira tells my father about the baby he helped to
make—due in a month—and my father is thrilled.

"Maybe we should start calling you Sire-a," he jokes.

"Anything you like," Ira says.

"What a wonderful arrangement," Dad says. "And with
so many parents, that child is going to feel so loved."

Once they finish talking about the baby, they talk
about my mother. Ira's heard so much about her.

"What was she like, Joe?" Ira asks.

"Drop-dead gorgeous," Dad answers. "Just a great gal."

"So compared to all these other ladies you've been
dating?"

"No equal," he says. "All of them but Doreen have been
problematic."

"Why don't you give us the whole lowdown," Ira says.

Now, I suddenly want to scream "No!" But I take a long
sip of my martini instead.

"That would take all night," Dad laughs.

"Give us the abridged version," Ira says.

"Well, let's see," Dad says. "Mini was anything but."

"Overweight, huh?" Ira says.

"To say the least. It wore thin with her pretty fast, no
pun intended."

"Who else, Joe?"

"Frieda was quixotic. Rita was neurotic."

"And Anita was despotic?" Ira adds.

"In a manner of speaking," Dad says. "Then there was Edie. She wouldn't commit."

"And Florence?" I ask.

Dad sighs. "Ach, no," he says. "Thankfully it's all past tense, because Doreen, the lady I'm with now, is the closest I've met to my wife. A lovely person, and she's kept her figure. Good dancer, tennis player, and she likes to sing with me, just like Ethel did."

"I hear she wears a wig," Ira says.

"That's Bobby's problem, not mine," Dad says.

"Well," Ira says, "I look forward to meeting her."

Then he excuses himself to use the men's room, walking away in his perfectly cut black blazer. Dad leans over, takes my hand.

"What a terrific guy," he whispers. "Perfect for you in every way."

I feel a tingle of pleasure go up my spine. "You think so, Dad?"

"I feel like I now have three sons instead of two. I couldn't be happier for you."

I should tell him how much it means to me to hear that. But "Thanks, Dad" is all I manage as I pull my hand out from under his. After dessert, as we're about to leave, an older lady who looks to be of means stops by the table. I have become so used to being Dad's pimp that I start assessing her, from soft copper hair to alligator bag. I can tell she's got her eye on him. I can also see she's had work done on her face, which is smooth as a plastic nectarine. Then I realize I'm wasting my powers of assessment.

He's got eyes only for Doreen now. What a relief he's off the market.

"I just had to tell you what nice-looking sons you have," this woman says to Dad.

Ira and I exchange looks. Then I look down at my plate, embarrassed.

"Yes," Dad says, not bothering to correct her. "Aren't they terrific?"

## CHAPTER 3

# Florida with Feeling

Six months later now, our plane has landed at Palm Beach airport, and I'm stepping off my flight just as I have for dozens of years. The airport crowd is the same—same tan faces of a certain age, same old pastel cardigans, Bermuda shorts, and golf caps on bald heads. Same looks of expectation on snowbird parents waiting for youngsters to get off the plane and make them proud. But something has changed for me. I am not stepping off the plane (among all the young couples and families) as the alienated single adult this weekend. Today I am here with Ira, my princely prize in an alligator shirt. I am a husband, or something like one.

We're planning to stay in Dad's apartment. He is to stay with Doreen for the long weekend. Ira would never make this kind of arrangement—a whole weekend with

my father and his new love? It's potentially treacher-
ous—four opinionated pushy people thrown into a first
weekend together, a double-dating demolition derby. No
wonder I'm anxious. But as the newly evolved me, the
*better* me, I firmly believe that I won't fall back into the
old cynical toxic patterns around my father. Today I'm a
man, a son, and a husband. And I am not here to criticize
or judge. I am not even here for reconciliation or meaning. I'm here to love, to be loved, and to get a tan, in that
order, and that's all.

We pick up the rental car—and it's the same style of
white Sebring convertible I had when I drove Dad on his
date with Edie. Except now I've got Ira at my side, fiddling
with his BlackBerry. There are all kinds of things I want
to tell him. So it's very annoying that his first impulse
is to look at his e-mail rather than at me or the lovely,
wide waterway sparkling under the bridge. But now that
we've been living together for a while, I have started to
understand the value of self-restraint, rather than saying
every stupid little thing that comes into my head. I try to
listen and just let him be. This is what it means to move
together as a couple, to ebb and flow, give and take, cha-
cha-cha, like my parents in those old home movies, halt-
ing, awkward, and attentive. So instead of sniping at him
to put away the BlackBerry and enjoy the damn view, I
pull over and figure out how to get the convertible top to
go down. He puts on his expensive sunglasses and looks
up. Even without a tan, he's handsome and aristocratic—
so Palm Beach, maybe Hollywood, too—and perfect for
the setting.

"This is fabulous," he says, then goes back to work. I
drive us the scenic way, and feel proud—as if it's my own

turf—of the sapphire ocean, Spanish mansions, rows of royal palms—slender as socialites—that sway above Ocean Boulevard. He appreciates it all, then he continues e-mailing. When we pull into the parking lot of my father's white wedding cake of a building, he looks up and nods, impressed with the 1950s architecture. "I love buildings like this," he declares. "They're such modern classics."

I don't see the architecture when I look up at this building. I just see my mother, who used to wait for me in a housedress on the fourth-floor walkway that looked down over the parking lot. And I see myself up there with her, trying to cheer her up, upgrade her look and her outlook. She refused to exercise. And I just kept nagging her about it straight through to the end. My brother never spoke to her as harshly as I did. But I didn't know how else to motivate her. I honestly thought that if she could just keep walking, then she wouldn't become so dependent on us for help. It took me a long time to realize that all she really needed was unconditional support, not coaching and criticism. Why couldn't I give it? And was it right to feel such relief at her deathbed? All these questions rush over me in waves as I pull up to this apartment building.

The doorman in the white-tiled lobby has our names. As we get into the elevator, I am seized with worries. Will my father embarrass me in front of Ira? Will Aunt Sylvia approve of him? Will I stop concerning myself with Doreen's wig and start focusing on what's beneath it? Most important, will my father make good on his solemn promise to shack up with her for the weekend so we can be alone in his apartment? And did he have the cleaning lady come today, as promised? I hope he'll be on his best behavior. Will I, for that matter? The last thing I need Ira to see is one of Dad's rage storms brought on by my cynicism.

No. That was the *old* me, I tell myself in an attempt to staunch the flow of anxieties. Nothing is going to faze me now that I am in love.

"But, Dad, you said you'd be staying with Doreen all weekend," I am hissing a half hour later, when it becomes clear he will not be clearing out of his apartment for us.

"Yes, but she has a friend visiting her now," he says.

I can actually feel my scalp tingling, my face flushing with rage. "How did this happen? We talked about it twice before we booked our flight."

"Come on, Bobby. What's your worry? I won't be in your way."

I had promised Ira that, if he came down here, we'd be staying alone. It was the way I could offer a weekend with Dad without being on top of him. Now, in this snug two-bedroom apartment that I thought we would have as our private aerie with a water view, we have a Joe Morris view. It feels like we're in the galley of a very small boat on a somewhat unpleasant sea. In ill-fitting cardigan and khakis and beige vinyl slip-ons, Dad hobbles from bedroom to kitchen with teabag hanging out of ceramic mug. He sits in front of the TV for ball games and news shows, expecting us to join him so he can have conversations during commercials. His cell phone is constantly going with the "Mexican Hat Dance" ring tone. His bridge magazines clutter the bathroom. Used toothpicks garnish the vanity. I had wanted to protect Ira from all this and not let him see how annoyed I can get. The big, evolved Bob who touched down an hour ago is now one little pissy Bobby on the verge of a tantrum.

Is this what happens to every child in the orbit of his parents?

"I'm so sorry for his mess," I tell Ira on the balcony. "It's bad, I know."

"No worse than yours," he replies. "And he closes his closet doors."

"I'm learning to close doors. I'm not this messy!"

"Don't kid yourself. I look at this apartment, and I see I've married your father."

I feel as if I've been hit in the face with a pie and a re-alization at the same time. I know I look like the old man. I know I sing like him. But in terms of everything else, aren't we as different as any father and son could be?

"Let's go find a hotel, my treat," I say. "This is going to end badly."

"Don't be such a drama queen," Ira says. "Stop project-ing. It is what it is."

"Aren't you the self-actualized little houseguest," I say.

"Do I have any choice?" he replies.

I really should be in a worse mood than I am. My fa-ther's little margarine tubs of dried fruit soaking in wine are on the kitchen counters, and his Styrofoam contain-ers of rancid leftovers from early-bird specials are in the fridge. His freebie newspapers, bank statements, bridge scores, and half-written letters are covering every sur-face of the living room, while his politically unsupport-able news shows blare throughout the apartment, and the phone calls are so constant you'd think he was running the office of recreation for the entire municipality of Palm Beach. It's not pretty, not at all. But with Ira right at

my side witnessing the whole hilarious debacle, how can
I be annoyed? My father is doing everything he can to
welcome us. He leaves us cleanish towels. He remembers
to leave no socks on the living room floor. He makes us
coffee in the morning, and although it's way too weak, we
appreciate the gesture.

"I love having you here with me," he says. "What a
thrill."

The next morning, Dad wants to take us to breakfast
at a motel with an oceanfront deck, a surprisingly nice
choice for someone who isn't partial to the majesty of
nature. We choose a big table closest to the beach. The
surf is so picturesque today—2 percent–skim foam waves
are frothing against wheat-toast sand. Ira fills Dad in on
the baby he helped make, a little girl named June, whom
we see a couple times a week. Dad gives us unsolicited
legal advice about the mortgage for the apartment we are
buying together. For a little while, the conversation is easy
and breakfast is breezy. Then it gets a little prickly, at least
for me. It isn't the shameless fascination Dad is showing
the bottle-blond waitress, grilling her about everything
from her education to her marital status. And it isn't the
fact that, as usual, he is playing games, saving money by
not ordering his own meal but sharing ours instead. It's
the agenda he has brought to this breakfast, an agenda I
thought we had put to rest weeks ago. He's soliciting Ira.
Doreen is having trouble finding an agent for her book
about Soviet Jews. It isn't that she can't write. She's been
published before. It's the topic, decidedly not hot.

"I wonder if the world has moved on from all that, Joe,"
says Ira, who was gracious enough to read some of the
manuscript.

"Look, she's family now," he told me at the time. "So I have to try."

Nothing came of it. *Dayenu*, as the Jews say. Enough. For anyone else that would be the end of the story. But Dad, who lives to be a useful adviser in all fields (even without experience in any of them), doesn't want to see Doreen frustrated. He has a new plan today, and a proposal, imperfectly typed on onion-skin paper. He hands it to Ira.

"The Second Hanukah?" Ira reads off the page. "A Soviet Jewry Story."

"I was hoping you'd be able to get this to Steven Spielberg," Dad says.

Ira takes a long drink from his coffee mug. He paces his response. "Second Hanukah, Joe?" he says. "Isn't an exodus more a Passover story?"

"Ira! Don't engage him," I say. "Steven Spielberg will *not* be interested."

"Let him talk, let him talk," Dad says.

"I can't believe you're still bugging Ira with this," I moan.

"Bobby, please, just let him talk!"

So I do, but it isn't easy. I mean, Ira is a generous person, and I appreciate that. But that doesn't mean he should get dragged into Doreen's publishing problems, too. And frankly, I don't know if I want to share him with someone so new to our lives. I really should be reaching over the table and crumbling up that movie pitch.

But Ira, typically so tough, is so sweet now, so solicitous, letting my father rattle on. So instead of making my own little pogrom and running Dad (along with Doreen's Soviet Jews) off this deck, I just listen and nod.

Why am I suddenly so sanguine? Maybe it's the cloudless Florida day and view of an ocean as infinite as the future I can see with Ira. Maybe it's the earnest tone of my well-meaning father, who just wants to help the lady he loves. Maybe the sun is frying my brain. The waves come in and go out, soothing and serene. I listen and drink my coffee. Ira keeps nodding. He loves me. So he loves my dad. Simple as that.

That night, we attend a dinner party at Doreen's place. Her building is nearby, a high-rise. She's on the ground floor. She greets us at the door warmly, with kisses, as if we've been part of the family forever. She wears an apron over her light blue slacks and blouse, a plain, midwestern look that reminds me of something my mother would have worn on a cool Florida night. The wig seems better now, or maybe I am.

"Come in," she says in a high-pitched flutter. "Let me show you around."

We say hello to her friend, Estelle, the houseguest who displaced my father this weekend. She is busy setting the table. Ira goes to help her. My father heads to the bathroom. Doreen takes off her apron and gives me a tour, proudly pointing out this sculpture from Africa and that painting from Israel. I find myself assessing things with a proprietary air, as if this apartment were the new annex to my family's territory. And since she owns and he rents, I have to assume that, in an effort to save some money next winter, he'll be moving in with her. Which means this may be where we'll be staying the next time we come down. It's almost impossible to imagine. But entirely plausible. And I actually kind of like this place. It's spacious and bright. The furniture is modern and unfussy. The books on her shelves are diverse and impressive. This is the home of a cultured woman. Photos of her family are framed in every room. They're sunny-looking people who could actually become family to me. My father has already reported that her kids are prosperous and trouble-free. Good. Who needs new issues in our family?

"This is the guest room," Doreen says. "You guys are welcome here anytime."

I stand in the door, eyeing a big pullout couch. It looks substantial enough to hold two people comfortably. And the room is big and well appointed. I check out her bedroom for only a moment, and barely step inside. Nice as it is, I'm too squeamish to look at the bed where my father has been sleeping with her this winter.

"I have lots of room for everyone here," she says. "I hope you'll come stay."

Something about this apartment feels familiar. It takes a while to figure it out, but by the time Doreen has led me to her living room and seated me on her couch, I realize what it is. Her home is decorated just like the one where I grew up, right down to the blue Chagall print on the wall.

Dad is sitting in an easy chair that reminds me of the one in our old living room. Doreen looks out from the kitchen and smiles at him as he relaxes in her home as if it were his own. A photograph of her deceased husband is on a bookshelf nearby, smiling down on us. My father is better looking, but not by much. "That's where your father sat the first time I had him over last winter," she tells me. "I was making him dinner, and I looked out into my living room and saw him sitting right there, feet up, reading my *Palm Beach Post*. He looked so at home, just like my husband, who loved this apartment. After that, I just knew he was the man for me."

I've been so self-absorbed that I haven't given her situation much thought until this moment. She is taking us all into her life as much as we are taking her into ours. Only instead of with doubt, she seems to be doing it with nothing but pleasure. Here is the place where she spent so many happy retirement years with her husband. They had had a long, good marriage, raised kids together, and were enjoying their golden years when he got sick. And suddenly she had on her hands what we had on ours with Mom. Except, in addition to worrying about an ailing man, she was also in the woman's role of cooking, cleaning, and doing all the things she did as a wife. She wanted to write books and articles. Instead, she had to care for a dying husband. It says a lot about her that she's so willing to throw herself back into love with a man Dad's age. He's several years older than she is and, with a heart giving him some trouble, not nearly as healthy.

"I just never thought I'd find someone who fit with me so well," she says.

"I'm very comfortable around you," Dad says.

"And I'm very comfortable around you, Joe," she replies.

"And what about when you're in his car?" I ask.

"Oy, the mess in that car," she sighs. "Don't get me started."

Old friends of my parents from Long Island join us for dinner. They knew Mom and Dad when they were young, and gave costume parties for Halloween and took dancing lessons at Arthur Murray. Others are friends of Doreen's, whom she is proud to introduce to us. It's a very assertive group, geeselike in vocal tone. I get grilled about journalism. Ira gets grilled about publishing. Doreen overcooks the roast, but it hardly matters. My father likes it well done. Ira and Aunt Sylvia get engaged in a lively conversation. It's strange to see the two of them together, and it still unmoors me to introduce people who have only known me as "Bobby" to my adult spouse. We drink many glasses of mediocre wine. Then we step outside for cigarettes.

"Is all this too much?" I ask Ira under a golf ball moon.

"Look, all these people are happy for you," he says. "So instead of worrying about me, why don't you just shut up and enjoy it."

"They're kind of adorable, aren't they?"

"Especially if you like hearing about their children."

"At least they didn't get out any manuscripts to show you."

"The night is still young."

Later, after the last guest departs, I look out from the kitchen to see my father and Doreen, sitting on the couch together, holding hands and talking quietly. He is bringing her hand to his face now, looking as blissful as I've ever seen him, at least since Mom was well. More than anything, he is a man who craves affection, and this is a woman who is not afraid to give it to him. And that's all he needs to make life complete.

It's chilly at midnight, but we leave the window in Dad's guest room open. As usual, Ira wants to snuggle, and scrambles to rest his head against my chest.

"Hold me," he whispers. It makes me anxious, with my father padding around right outside our door. But I do, and he slips off to sleep.

His head is a little heavy on me. He can keep me up nights with his snoring and snuggling. But I would be nowhere without it. I spent my entire adulthood avoiding affection. I'm not sure why. Maybe I associated vulnerability with weakness. Maybe I was trying to assert my autonomy because my mother never did with my father.

But I was missing everything.

Ira snores softly on my chest. In the next room I hear the operatic snoring of the other man in my life. Surround sound. A wind brushes the palm trees outside and they rattle. Then a train whistle blows its soulful sigh across the waterway.

I remember thirty-five years ago, my father was out on a cold spring night planting two sugar sap maple trees in our backyard. My brother and I were in the den, watching TV. He tried to get us to come out to help him. He wanted to share a nice moment with his sons. But we refused. Even then we questioned him. Why was he bothering? Years later, those trees had grown so big that they turned that little quarter-acre backyard into something like paradise. They towered over that yard, majestic presences that shaded us in summer and filled our suburban world with flaming colors in the fall. And my whole life, with all my aggravation with everything, I'd be able to sit in that yard in peace as the sounds of leaves rustled high above me in the wind. I'd nap, read, appreciate being alive for a while. It was just so comfortable to me, more than anywhere else in the world.

And that's how it is with Ira.

The next morning, we're on our way home. As our plane soars over Palm Beach before banking north, we look down at the little beach-fringed city below. I can

see us thirty years from now, down there on some balcony in a wedding-cake building, singing together and
complaining about our cataracts and gastritis. The truth
is we aren't young anymore. We like to think we're with
it because we keep up with the new music and hip TV
shows. We have young friends, and dress like people
half our age, and move freely in the world—unbur-
dened bachelors with opinions to throw around, along
with one child to show off occasionally in a stroller. But
with her, we're like doting old uncles. We have wrinkles
and silver hair now, and the truth is that there is more
behind us than ahead.

"Palm Beach seniors are a hoot," Ira says as he flips
through a duty-free brochure.

"So you enjoyed yourself?"

"It was utterly banal and utterly uplifting at the same
time."

"Should we think about retiring down here someday?"
I ask.

"Maybe," he says. "I guess I could see growing old with
you. Only you better lose ten pounds. I think you're getting way too comfortable with me."

What comes out of my mouth is as natural as breath.

"I love you," I tell him.

"You better," he says with a smirk. "Because I'm the
best thing that's ever happened to you."

## CHAPTER 4

# End Where It Started

It's several months later, a year and a half after my mother died, and my father and I are going to visit her grave again. But first, a tour of the past, a drive down memory lane. In his cluttered car that smells a little rank, we cruise the old suburb. Today I'm not finding it as unattractive as I used to. Or is it that I need a new prescription for my glasses? We visit the library where my mother worked for thirty years. It used to look so ungainly and modern. Now it looks comfortable with itself, stately and purposeful, with ivy growing on brick walls. Inside, under a high, renovated ceiling flooded with light, we look at the desk where she sat with the reference books and microfiche machines she knew so well. She was a core of this library, a reliable face for everyone who used the place. And a pretty good shusher, too. Shhh! Dad is trying to tell the staff all about her now. They're young and look at him with blank stares. Nobody remembers who she was or even recognizes her name. I tell him they're very busy and to leave them alone. But can't they even pretend to be interested? Has it really been that long since she retired?

Around the corner, our house has been fixed up by new owners. There's elegant landscaping now, ornamental trees and shrubs where there used to be scraggly pines. A tasteful porch has been added to the front. Somebody has seen our house as we never saw it and has put an effort into bringing it up to a level my parents could never imagine. The whole neighborhood looks nicer than I remember, with wide streets bordered by canals and the bright expanse of Great South Bay all around that I took for granted for so many years.

"Why did I dislike it so much?" I ask. "Why was I so unhappy here?"

Dad doesn't know. And I can't say I'll ever know either. I've always been insecure, and I've always liked to complain. And without anything important to complain about, I guess I needed something, anything, to pick on for all those years. But now I think I'm finally tired of my unhappiness. Maybe all it takes is an adjustment, a decision, like when you stop looking for perfection in a mate and finally fall in love. Maybe happiness isn't as alien to me as I had thought. Isn't it in my DNA? Look at my father.

At the end of our old street, he makes a left turn onto the Montauk Highway. We pass rows of medical buildings. We pass the road to the high school. I feel like I'm a teenager again, cruising with a buddy with nothing but time on our hands.

"I didn't get much of an education here, but I guess I did okay," I say.

"You did great," he says.

"I don't know about that."

"It's just a matter of how you look at things, Bobby," he replies, as he hugs the center line and makes me grip my seat. "Besides, where you're from doesn't mean a thing. Look how well you've done. You can go as far as you want with your life."

He's said this to me since I can remember. But for the first time, I hear it.

What do fathers do for sons? Most of them know they have to be providers. Many of them bond over tennis or golf or fishing trips. Some leave their sons a business. Others leave governments in their hands or create political legacies that can put them in the White House. Some, like Daedalus, are too ambitious, and make their sons fly, like Icarus, too close to the sun. Others are impossible to please. Not my father, my biggest fan, who revels in my life. Finally, as I look into the near future of my own old age, I can see that it isn't the quality of all those observations or suggestions he is so anxious to share that matters. What matters is the sincerity of the intention, his pleasure in participating in life with me. Even without a father of his own, he has figured out how to express his affection fully, one of the hardest things to do for men of his generation. He has encouraged me to speak up and sing out, unashamed. He has made me see the importance of demanding romance from life, regardless of how elusive. He has showed me that it's okay to be vulnerable and a little foolish. He has taught me half of the songs in my repertoire and several pretty good dirty jokes, too. Not bad.

We drive west on the industrial Route 109, into the late-afternoon sun, and then pull into Mount Ararat Cemetery, passing rows of identical gravestones before he parks his car. This time we don't get lost when we walk to Mom's grave. Maybe it's the weather or time of year. Maybe it's all the Sudafed I had to take this morning. Or maybe it's being in love and knowing my father is, too. For whatever the reason, this time I can't dismiss this place with such a critical eye. It doesn't seem unattractive to me now. The trees are blooming in shades of yellow, pink, and white, and it's very pretty.

"You know, Dad," I say as we stop at my mother's grave, now with grass fully grown in around it, "I was just thinking, maybe I will be buried here with you after all."

Dad looks surprised. "But I thought you don't like all the traffic noise," he says.

"I don't," I say. "But since I'll be dead, maybe it won't bother me so much."

He laughs. "Good point."

"Yeah, I'll be buried here if your offer still stands, but you know that there's going to have to be room for more than just me."

He breaks into a smile.

"I was hoping you'd say that, because I just signed for a plot for Ira here, too," he says. "So now we can all be together at the end for a nice long visit."

"Perfect. Thank you, Dad."

We're quiet for a moment, basking in something that I'd have to say is contentment. One old man, one middle-aged one, finally settling in together. We stare down at my mother's grave. The budding maple tree branches over us bow in the breeze.

"Those last years were so hard," I say.

"I wish I could have done better for her," he replies. "I just didn't know how."

I feel the old resentment for a moment. Then I think of my mother, right here with us. And just like that, I let it go. It wasn't his way to worry, to be dutiful every moment of their marriage. She was the reliable one, like my brother. He was the fun one, the one who made her life amusing—irritating, never dull.

"You know what, Dad? You did the best you could do."

"So did you, Bobby, so did you."

He leans over and puts his arm around me. Then he leans in for one of his bonding bear hugs. This time I don't squirm. I turn and face him, and I open my arms and take him in. His cheek feels smooth against mine. His hair soft against my forehead. His chest expands and contracts. After we pull apart, he's quiet. Then, just like he does each time we're here, he looks down at my mother's grave to serenade her. "Honey," he says. "This one's for you."

*When somebody loves you*
*It's no good unless he loves you*
*All the way.*

His voice shakes a little. He doesn't quite have the breath he used to. But as always, his pitch is perfect, and his delivery is smooth as any crooner's.

*Happy to be near you*
*When you need someone to cheer you*
*All the way.*

He lets the lyrics linger in the air, then he turns to
me.

"You know this song, Bobby," he says. "Why don't you
sing with me?"

So I sing with him, hesitantly at first, then with more
conviction. Our voices wrap in harmony, twisting together, and as indistinguishable as a couple of blackbirds
in a tree.

*Taller than the tallest tree is,*
*That's how it's got to feel;*
*Deeper than the deep blue sea is,*
*That's how deep it goes,*
*If it's real.*

Suddenly seized with the thought of how shocked my
mother would be to see the two of us getting along so well,
I laugh. Then emotion wells up inside—grief, happiness,
and everything in between, and my eyes fill with tears.
My father puts his arm around me, holds me close.

*Who knows where the road will lead us?*
*Only a fool would say.*
*But if you let me love you,*
*It's for sure I'm going to love you*
*All the way.*

When it's time to go, we walk along the pebbled cemetery path and get back into his car to head home to the brand-new lives we have ahead of us. We're going our separate ways. Yet we've never been closer. Then I sit down in the passenger seat, and, as he starts the engine, I put my brand-new, four-hundred-dollar, brown suede Prada loafer into a half-eaten tuna salad sandwich, heavy on the mayo.

"Dad! What is this?"

"Don't throw it out," he says. "I'll have it later."